H ERE

HERE'S ME HERE

Further reflections of a Lapsed Protestant

GLENN PATTERSON

NEW ISLAND

HERE'S ME HERE

First published in 2015
by New Island Books,
16 Priory Hall Office Park,
Stillorgan,
County Dublin,
Republic of Ireland.

www.newisland.ie

PRINT ISBN: 978-1-84840-446-5
EPUB ISBN: 978-1-84840-456-4
MOBI ISBN: 978-1-84840-455-7

British Library Cataloguing Data.
A CIP catalogue record for this book is available from the British Library.

Typeset by JVR Creative India
Cover design by Mariel Deegan
Printed by ScandBook AB

New Island received financial assistance from The Arts Council (*An Chomhairle Ealaíon*), 70 Merrion Square, Dublin 2, Ireland.

10 9 8 7 6 5 4 3 2 1

For Em and Ger

Contents

Here

After decades of conflict, and a few years carrying on like new lovers coy about the names for the bits that give them pleasure, after negotiations lasting, as negotiations are bound to last, long, long into the night, politicians of all parties have agreed that the name of this place shall henceforward be ... 'Here'. Citizens shall be 'people here', the remainder of the island 'down there' and the island to the east of us 'over there'. The United States becomes 'way over there'.

Please note, though, people down there, over there, and especially way over there may entertain some very strange notions about people here.

Anna Lo, Northern Ireland's first representative of Chinese extraction, tells a story. She was at a reception in Washington.

'I think you must have wandered into the wrong place,' a man said.

'No, I'm in the right place.'

'But this is a reception for ...'

'I know what it's a reception for,' she said. 'I was handpicked to come.'

'Handpicked?'

'Picked, by hand.'

'You?'

'Me. But what about you?'

'Oh, my family left during the Great Hunger, eighteen-and-forty ...'

'No, I meant where do you pay your taxes?'

'Well, here, of course.'

He meant 'there' of course, way over there, where they were. She said to him, 'Well, I pay mine back there.' She meant here.

Because that's where she's from.

Here.

Short Cuts, Radio 4, January 2012

Found in France

I have never subscribed to the view that you have to go away to find yourself. I have never even been able to write the phrase without thinking of something my father-in-law said about a feckless relative, how he had found himself all right, with both hands. Then again I have never been all that good at going away.

(I lived in England for a few years, but – sorry to disappoint anyone for whom it is an article of political faith – England isn't 'away', it's over the fence.)

Holidays in our household are haphazard, last minute, and not in a bargain-online-deal sort of way. In fact budget airlines can afford to offer their rock-bottom fares precisely because there are people like my wife and me sitting in the middle of July looking for a flight to just about anywhere and resigned to paying just about anything.

This year we made sure we wouldn't be caught out and started making plans in the early New Year to go away with friends. Well-organised friends. Friends who within three days

3

of us floating the idea came back to us with the perfect gîte in Brittany, only to trump it a couple of days later with a perfect-gîte-with-Jacuzzi combo. (And the world, I realize, has shrunk to such a degree that 'gîte in Brittany' looks to most people's eyes how 'caravan in Tyrella' did to mine growing up. 'Jacuzzi' looks plain B&Q-y.) Friends who even sent us details of the car-hire options at Rennes–Saint-Jacques Airport. Sent us everything in the end bar the luggage labels to tie to our lapels: 'If found looking disoriented please direct to …'

So anyway, August came and we went. One whole week. (Our friends had booked an extra week camping with some other well-organised people they knew.) And do you know what? I did find myself. Or at least found out some things about myself that had not been apparent up till then. That I am skinny was not one of them, although it was pointed out to me several times on the beach, by people who I imagine would never dream of saying to someone, 'Man but you are *fat*.' (Anyone ever asks me how I stay so thin, I tell them the truth: drugs. Lots and lots of drugs.)

Principally I found out this: if the child is father of the man, as Wordsworth has it, then I must have been adopted by the eleven-year-old with my name who used to run around Finaghy in the early 1970s, writing 'FTP' on lampposts, bus stops, park benches and other street furniture.

It was our last night in the gîte. The camping friends had already arrived and pitched their tent in a field out back in preparation for the next week's adventures. There were children everywhere, adoptive fathers and mothers of as yet unimaginable men and women. There was an approximate half-tonne of sardines, washed and gutted (boy, were they gutted), on the kitchen draining board. There was a brick-built barbecue to be lit. I took the kitchen matches and walked round the side of the house, because, another thing I discovered, for all my garrulousness, my first to the bar and what's everybody having,

4

I am not that sociable a person. It suited me to be outside on my own for a while, building my elaborate sardine pyre. Which of course (and, yes, apologies, you really have read this far only to find yourself in a man-fails-to-light-barbecue tale) failed to ignite. And I thought there was just no way this should be happening. Not because I fancy myself as an alpha male (see beach comments above), but because I am a bred-in-the-bone Northern Irish *Protestant* male, whose adolescence, in between scribbling 'FTP' and playing football, was largely taken up with burning things. Time was I could have set a wet stick on fire just by looking at it.

Maybe I wasn't drunk enough. Maybe the gift of fire always left me and my mates at the end of July – crossed Finaghy Bridge for the Internment Night bonfires – and we just never knew it.

In the end I got on my hands and knees and blew. And blew; blew until pretty much everything that had been in me was in there among the charcoal and paper spills, proving some third-form chemistry experiment and producing, at what felt as though it must be the end of my life, a flame.

By the time the sardines came I had rolled off my knees on to my hunkers, and was taking a pull on my beer.

'No problems getting it going then?' said well-organised friend #1.

To which of course I replied:

'...'

You need breath to tell a barefaced lie. And just a little more neck maybe than the man that child-me fathered ever grew. (Though he grew just enough, thank you, to write one.)

News Letter, 8 September 2007

Here We Are

Where do you turn at times like these?

The answer for most people is probably not to novels. More's the pity. I would say that, being a novelist myself, but bear with me. A novel, my contemporary Robert McLiam Wilson once wrote, is 'shoe-swapping on the grand scale'. To read one is to engage in repeated acts of empathy, to accept the invitation to see the world as it appears to people other than oneself.

Imagine, the novel says, line by line, page after page. *Keep imagining.*

China Miéville in *The City and the City* imagines two cities – Beszel and Ul Qoma – inhabiting the same geographical space. Some streets are 'total' – wholly in one city or the other – some are 'alter' – now in this city, now in that – and the remainder are 'crosshatched' – in both cities at once. Citizens of Beszel and their Ul Qoman counterparts are trained from birth, on pain of punishment, not to see the 'aliens' in their midst. But still, on occasion, 'breaches' occur, often violently.

Miéville doesn't say whether Beszel or Ul Qoma has a Christmas market, but he might otherwise have been describing the *cities* of Belfast in recent days.

Time and again the words come over the airwaves: 'no one sees us, no one is listening to us.' The will of the 'majority' is variously — often contradictorily — invoked.

Of course, we have a system here whereby the actual will of the majority can be periodically measured. It involves citizens going to a polling station and making a mark on a ballot paper. If the candidate beside whose name they make their mark does not do what he or she promised, they have the opportunity next time around to put their mark elsewhere.

In most democracies this leaves open the possibility that at regular intervals another party will form a government. In Northern Ireland for the foreseeable future the likelihood is that the exercise will return the same mandatory coalition of DUP and Sinn Féin that has — I hesitate to say *served* us — since 2006. 'Hesitate to say' because much blame for the current mess must be laid at the door of the DUP, along with individual members of the Unionist Party, for the distribution of those inflammatory leaflets in the run-up to the Belfast City Council 'flag' vote at the start of this month, blaming the Alliance Party for the Union flag's being 'ripped down' from City Hall.

Peter Robinson's response to the riots and the death threat to Alliance MP Naomi Long, as he stood beside Hillary Clinton in Parliament Buildings, was as egregious an example of political hand-washing as you could wish (make that 'hope never again') to see. 'Our journey is irreversible,' he said. 'We are determined to go on and while from time to time we will have setbacks there is no linear progression to a stable and peaceful society.'

Never mind linear progression, there is no sense at all in his words of agency; no recognition that the 'setbacks' might have been at least in part engineered by the party that Mr Robinson leads.

To this extent his words were perfectly in keeping with political rhetoric here in recent years. Our politicians may not have mastered the art of speaking out of both sides of their mouths at once, but a good many of them a good deal of the time are adept at saying one thing out of one side and very quickly after something entirely different out of the other, goading political opponents – or sometimes the 'other lot' generally – then taking cover in the platitudes of the Peace Process.

The playground equivalent is hitting someone a dig then hiding behind the teacher.

In part this is a problem with the Process itself. The open-endedness coded into the word has long since ceased to be enabling and become destabilising: 'we', or 'they' (depending on your politics), it seems to say, are not finished yet.

I don't know about anyone else, but I thought that what I was voting for back in 1998 was an agreement. Yes, peace has to be worked at, but – guess what? – peace always has to be worked at, everywhere. It's called respect for your fellow human beings, and, dare I say it, empathy.

We need to demand the same standards of ourselves as we expect of others. (Try this for instance: if it does not dilute anyone's Britishness to have the Union Flag flown on designated days neither should it dilute anyone's Irishness to call this place Northern Ireland?)

We need to make sure we do not take pleasure in the discomfort of others.

We need to take responsibility for the rights of others.

We need to imagine not a future but a *present* for us all beyond endless Process.

Politicians – voters – here is where we are. Now, deal with it.

Belfast Telegraph, 18 December 2012

Luxus

Luxus *m* – luxury
Collins German-English Dictionary

✿

'Brothers and sisters the time has come for each and every one
of you to decide whether you are going to be the problem or
whether you are going to be the solution. You must choose
brothers. You must choose.'
MC5, 'Kick Out the Jams'

✷

'You've never been more beautiful/ your eyes like two full
moons/ than here in this poor old dancehall/ among the
dreadful tunes/ the awful songs we don't even hear ...'
Magnetic Fields, 'Nothing Matters When We're Dancing'

There used to be so many fish shops in Cold War East Berlin people fed the cheap fish to their cats.

What you think you know you don't.

A dead goldfish can be revived with a drop of whiskey or, if that fails, by mouth-to-mouth resuscitation.

Some of what you know you wish you didn't.

A barmaid arriving for work here one morning found a goldfish motionless on the floor. She popped it back into the tank above the bar – no whiskey, no mouth-to-mouth. The goldfish came round, though for days afterwards it would make sudden dashes towards the surface as though trying to leap out again.

I know a metaphor when I hear one. I know a fishy tale. I know enough not to mix them up. I do. I know I do ...

I am on a stool below the fish tank, mid-afternoon, midweek, month of March, my forty-fifth year. The Artist is behind me somewhere, preoccupied with tiles and tabletops and the ghost of last night's bums-on-seats. The Owner is at the far end of the counter, looking uncomfortable with the daylight. In the window to my right a twist of yellowed tubing hangs like something intestinal, an appendix maybe, left over with the tiles from the days when this was a kosher butcher's shop. (Just saying the words 'kosher butcher' in Berlin is to flicker-book through a whole century of horror.) At night this tubing gets a neon rocket up its arse and does its best Starry Plough impersonation as if to proclaim it is a country – a universe – unto itself in here.

Last night I sat until the stars blurred, over the shoulders of the Teacher Who Fell Off A Chair and the Diplomat's Son Who Sat On Che Guevara's Lap, and one for the road became two, became three, became drink and pray there is still ground beneath you when rise from your seat.

This afternoon, though, I am not looking *at* but *beyond*, to the crane lowering klieg lights from the penthouse across the way.

Prenzlauer Berg – for that is where we are, the Artist, the Owner, the goldfish doo-wopping at the waterline, and me, the Writer – Prenzlauer Berg is the German film industry's backdrop of choice just now. Prenzlauer Berg is an estate agent's wet dream. If it is luxury you are after you will find it in spades in Prenzlauer Berg.

Just don't come looking for it in here.

Luxus.

It is held together by Polyfilla and gaffer tape. You don't even want to think about the wiring. A bulb blows, that's it, gone, and who knows when it will be replaced. If.

Luxus.

It is Warhol. It is Dada. A whole fountain of inverted meaning. It drags luxury down from the penthouses, back through that little twisted tube hanging in the window. Think about this, it says. Think again.

✶

Jesus, in some medieval versions of the nativity, was born in a penthouse. The 'house' is a red herring; it is the 'pent' you need to focus on. The Middle English word is *pentis*: a lean-to, an add-on, an appendix.

✶

When I first went to Berlin in 1990 it was like a wall coming down in my understanding of Europe. It was like a wall coming down in my understanding of home. The city's own wall had been dismantled almost two years before, although in places it looked more like half an hour ago. Actually, never mind the Cold War, in places it looked like the Second World War had just ended. On the day I arrived I walked with the friend I was staying with across the no-man's-land of Potsdamer Platz,

11

Hitler's bunker to our left, the Brandenburg Gate beyond, and on out east, past buildings that were more bullet-hole than brick, to her flat in Prenzlauer Berg.

I had never walked so far across a city (I'm from Belfast, I had never had that much city to walk across), or cared so little about the distance. I had never been, have never been since, so excited by a city: its history, yes, but also its here and now. And nowhere felt more here and now than Prenzlauer Berg. It was in Prenzlauer Berg, around the Gethsemane Church, that resistance to the GDR had burgeoned and it was to Prenzlauer Berg after the regime collapsed that much of Berlin's alternative nightlife gravitated. Behind every shot-pocked tenement block, it seemed, was another courtyard – *hinterhof* – another staircase up to another one-room bar, or gallery or performance space, or bar, gallery, performance space rolled into one. I didn't get to bed until breakfast the next day. It was all so thrillingly ad hoc: provisional, I would have said if someone else hadn't already had a monopoly on the word.

I was living in Lisburn at the time and running a weekly writing group in Portadown Library. The group finished at nine o'clock. The last train to Lisburn came through at a quarter to ten, suspicious objects on the line outside Newry permitting. For half an hour or more every Wednesday I would sit in Portadown Station, on the border between the Protestant and Catholic ends of town, alert to every footfall, and curse the place for a god-bothering dump. I cursed Lisburn too. I cursed Belfast. I cursed them twice as roundly when I had to come back from Berlin.

If Berlin's wall could come down, why couldn't our walls?

Perhaps because (it didn't occur to me to think it back then) the citizens of Berlin hadn't asked in the first place for their wall to be put up, extended, reinforced by petrol bombs – or worse

– and by injunctions and judicial reviews over who could do what where and when.

Fifteen years on the only bits of the Berlin Wall left standing are monuments and outdoor museums. (At least that's one thing no one can teach us here in Northern Ireland, how to put up a memorial.) Out towards Wedding, where there was for a while in late '61 a literal window of opportunity for people wanting to escape west, until the buildings on the east of the wall were demolished, tram tracks are being laid up the middle of the 'death strip'. Potsdamer Platz, once the crossroads between the American, the British, and the Russian zones of occupation, is now home to a mega mall and cinema complex with landmark buildings for Daimler-Chrysler and Sony. Not far away, near Alexanderplatz, where on 4 November 1989 a million people gathered to protest against the old regime, the Ideal Worker looks bewildered, as if he has awoken from decades-long sleep to find he is no longer a colossus but a buffoon: a pavement ranter, a bottom pincher. The Institute of Marxism-Leninism, on the border of Mitte and Prenzlauer Berg, is as derelict as a seventies' Belfast cinema. (My own childhood cinema, closed since 1975, has just been reincarnated as Tivoli Court Apartments.) I want to draw an arrow pointing east from the Institute a couple of thousand miles: business as usual, contact Kim Jong-il. Actually, I want to catch myself on, and start saving now to buy property in Pyongyang. One nation's *post-* is another nation's *pre-*.

Fifteen years on, Prenzlauer Berg has lost some of its old identity. No longer a borough in its own right, it was recently re-designated one of thirteen 'localities' of Pankow. The word on the street, and in the bars, these days is improvement, not improvisation. Or at least that is the official word, but there is still dissent, if you keep your eyes and ears open. On Schönhauser Allee someone has taken the trouble to climb to the top of the scaffolding around a building under renovation and write, 'Fuck the Free World'.

And then there is Luxus.

✳

Luxus is Latin for 'dislocated'. You can find a bit of it in ineluctable, that which cannot be escaped.

✳

The Artist has a friend – the Critic – who has a flat off a *hinterhof* on Kollwitzstrasse and who has, in his turn, a friend upstairs with a bed where I can sleep. The Friend's place is not so much a flat as a flat-sized hi-fi: a state of the art within a state. He has built the system himself, from components bought and bartered and salvaged down the years. It was either that, he suggests, or carrying on drinking as he used to, alcohol in the GDR being as cheap as chips ... or fish. He tells me how in those days he used to smuggle his reel-to-reel tape recorder through the streets to friends' flats to record illicit LPs. He tells me that was how he first heard *Kick Out the Jams* by Detroit's MC5. His expression tells me the rest: this was true revolution. I begin to think I can never have really listened to the MC5, as opposed to listening to stories about them (proto-punks, White Panthers). My expression must tell him this. When I get in from Luxus the afternoon of the klieg lights I find on my pillow a copy of the CD he has burned, complete with colour printout of the sleeve, Rob Tyner double-exposed on the back, hollering into the mike.

He is hollering now as I write this, 'I'm at my borderline, I'm at my borderline ...' and for a moment I'm at Portadown Station all those Wednesday nights ago, on edge.

Back in the bar that night it is Magnetic Fields on the sound system, *69 Love Songs*: a quieter subversion (note, not 68 or 70 Love Songs). The appendix has turned to plough again in the window, the world beyond so much fog. (On our way here I lost sight of the Artist somewhere around Prenzlauer Berg's famous Water Tower then saw a flash in the murk: some idea he had had about trees.) The Teacher Who Fell Off A Chair is in again and the Diplomat's Son Who Sat On Che Guevara's Lap. It is always a balancing act, that dependency of customer on bar, bar on customer: who will blink, or change, first?

Magnetic Fields have arrived at somewhere in the low fifties of their repertoire, 'The Death of Ferdinand de Saussure': 'We don't know anything, you don't know anything, I don't know anything about love.'

Saussure was the father of structuralism. What I know about structuralism could be scratched on the short end of a brick: signifier and signified, binary oppositions ...

Male implies female, dark, light, communism ... what?

When I ask the Owner later that night what he was thinking, opening a bar whose upkeep he occasionally seems indifferent, even hostile, to, he shrugs and says, 'I just wanted there to be a place where I could go.' It doesn't seem that extravagant a luxury in a city of three and a half million, in a neighbourhood of a couple of hundred thousand. And I remember how after my first visit to Berlin I became obsessed with the idea of opening a bar in Belfast. A friend and I had it all planned. We would take over the down-at-heel Du Barry's Saloon Bar near the Albert Clock. The Humanist, we were going to call it, for the four weeks it would have lasted before we went bankrupt. We wouldn't *do* an awful lot to it. There was too much being done to bars as it was. (Du Barry's was comprehensively done to a few years later.) Still, we might have changed a light bulb.

The Owner doesn't tell me that he was jailed under the old regime for refusing to work. He doesn't tell me either what he thinks looking past his small constellation of lights at the luxury apartments across the way, but I think I can guess.

The opposite of all that went before is not this.

✳

Appendix One

White Panther Party 10-Point Program

1. Full endorsement and support of Black Panther Party's 10-Point Program.
2. Total assault on the culture by any means necessary, including rock 'n' roll, dope, and fucking in the streets.
3. Free exchange of energy and materials – we demand the end of money!
4. Free food, clothes, housing, dope, music, bodies, medical care – everything free for everybody!
5. Free access to information media – free the technology from the greed creeps!
6. Free time and space for all humans – dissolve all unnatural boundaries!
7. Free all schools and all structures from corporate rule – turn the buildings over to the people at once!
8. Free all prisoners everywhere – they are our brothers!
9. Free all soldiers at once – no more conscripted armies!
10. Free the people from their 'leaders' – leaders suck – all power to all the people! Freedom means free everyone!

— John Sinclair, Minister of Information, White Panther Party, November 1st, 1968

(John Sinclair managed the MC5 until 1969, when he was sentenced to ten years for possession of two joints. The band subsequently distanced themselves from his statements urging violence.)

Appendix Two

69 Love Songs
1. Absolutely Cuckoo — 1:34
2. I Don't Believe in the Sun — 4:16
3. All My Little Words — 2:46
4. A Chicken with Its Head Cut Off — 2:41
5. Reno Dakota — 1:05
6. I Don't Want to Get Over You — 2:22
7. Come Back from San Francisco — 2:48
8. The Luckiest Guy on the Lower East Side — 3:43
9. Let's Pretend We're Bunny Rabbits — 2:25
10. The Cactus Where Your Heart Should Be — 1:11
11. I Think I Need a New Heart — 2:32
12. The Book of Love — 2:42
13. Fido, Your Leash is Too Long — 2:33
14. How Fucking Romantic — 0:58
15. The One You Really Love — 2:53
16. Punk Love — 0:58
17. Parades Go By — 2:56
18. Boa Constrictor — 0:58
19. A Pretty Girl is Like ... — 1:50
20. My Sentimental Melody — 3:07
21. Nothing Matters When We're Dancing — 2:27
22. Sweet-Lovin' Man — 4:59

23. The Things We Did and Didn't Do – 2:11
24. Roses – 0:27
25. Love is Like Jazz – 2:56
26. When My Boy Walks Down the Street – 2:38
27. Time Enough for Rocking When We're Old – 2:03
28. Very Funny – 1:26
29. Grand Canyon – 2:28
30. No One Will Ever Love You – 3:14
31. If You Don't Cry – 3:06
32. You're My Only Home – 2:17
33. (Crazy for You But) Not That Crazy – 2:18
34. My Only Friend – 2:01
35. Promises of Eternity – 3:46
36. World Love – 3:07
37. Washington, D.C. – 1:53
38. Long-Forgotten Fairytale – 3:37
39. Kiss Me Like You Mean It – 2:00
40. Papa Was a Rodeo – 5:01
41. Epitaph for My Heart – 2:50
42. Asleep and Dreaming – 1:53
43. The Sun Goes Down and the World Goes Dancing – 2:46
44. The Way You Say Good-Night – 2:44
45. Abigail, Belle of Kilronan – 2:00
46. I Shatter – 3:09
47. Underwear – 2:49
48. It's a Crime – 3:54
49. Busby Berkeley Dreams – 3:36
50. I'm Sorry I Love You – 3:06
51. Acoustic Guitar – 2:37
52. The Death of Ferdinand de Saussure – 3:10
53. Love in the Shadows – 2:54
54. Bitter Tears – 2:51
55. Wi' Nae Wee Bairn Ye'll Me Beget – 1:55

56. Yeah! Oh, Yeah! – 2:19
57. Experimental Music Love – 0:29
58. Meaningless – 2:08
59. Love is Like a Bottle of Gin – 1:46
60. Queen of the Savages – 2:12
61. Blue You – 3:03
62. I Can't Touch You Anymore – 3:05
63. Two Kinds of People – 1:10
64. How to Say Goodbye – 2:48
65. The Night You Can't Remember – 2:17
66. For We Are the King of the Boudoir – 1:14
67. Strange Eyes – 2:01
68. Xylophone Track – 2:47
69. Zebra – 2:15

Appendix Three

Localities of Pankow

Blankenburg
Blankenfelde
Buch
Französisch Buchholz
Heinersdorf
Karow
Niederschönhausen
Pankow
Prenzlauer Berg
Rosenthal
Stadtrandsiedlung Malchow
Weißensee
Wilhelmsruh

Appendix Four

Portadown Station

Footfall
12,000 pw

Sex
49% – M
51% – F

Social-Economic
AB – 34%
CI – 37%
C2 – 18%
DE – 11%

Employment Status
Employed – 70%
Student – 17%
Housewife – 3%
Other – 10%

Frequency of use
Daily – 43%
Weekly – 29%
Less Often – 28%

Copyright Onscreen Solutions

Appendix Five

24 November 2006

The slogan on the posters might have come straight from my early nineties nightmares. 'Don't Cross the Line', it reads, above a graphic of a car trapped on a level crossing. The view across the line from platform one appears little changed: same ferns, same row of rooftops, same aerials angled towards the distant Denny factory sign, around which the same inexplicable steam billows. But the waiting room now has a plasma screen above the ticket booths with ads for Rushmere Shopping Centre, Craigavon Borough Council, Chestnut Lodge. The straplines bleed into one another: 'Something for – something to suit – everyone ... no one feels left out.' Inclusiveness is the new exclusiveness. Second-class has been written off, or at least written out of the script. In this world of Passenger's Charters and Independent Monitoring Results on reliability, punctuality, and speed in picking up the phone, of leaf-fall leaflets and improved cross-border service, we are none of us lower than enterprise class, even if those that were first are not now last, but just first plus.

In a break between the ads the plasma screen treats us in our percentages (see Appendix Four) to archive footage of a Model T Ford with DIY propellers on the roof. The blades turn silently, furiously, but the Model T never leaves the ground. All the while a news-bar rolls across the bottom of the screen, 'Assembly to meet', 'Baghdad bomb victims buried', 'Wagon Wheels firm for sale'.

I walk out of the station (High Street Mall, Magowan West, Matalan to my right) a little before eleven o'clock, so never discover how the plasma screen – the waiting room – copes with Michael Stone wedged in a revolving door at Stormont shouting 'No Sell Out Paisley'. I carry on through the underpass to where I parked my car, trying not to give credence to the lines scrawled on the walls.

'Fuck Ulster' (talk about a lack of ambition), 'Shoot all Huns'.

Appendix Six

Googliography

White Panthers: http://www.luminist.org/archives/wpp.htm
Black Panthers: http://www.luminist.org/archives/bpp.htm
Plough and stars: http://www.geocities.com/Athens/Sparta/1648/ceacht_e.htm
Plasma ads: http://www.onscreensolutions.co.uk/home.asp
Structuralism: http://www.litencyc.com/php/stopics.php?rec=true&UID=122
Enterprise: http://www.translink.co.uk/enterpriseservices.asp
Appendicitis: http://www.medicinenet.com/appendicitis/article.htm

The author wishes to acknowledge Victor Sloan and the Millennium Court Arts Centre.

Photograph

I have been working off and on for a couple of years with an architect friend, Declan Hill, on an attempt to map the wall or rampart that in the seventeenth century surrounded the town of Belfast – or, at least, may have surrounded it. There is some debate about whether maps of the time show an existing structure or sketches for work never carried out. Declan and I meet occasionally to look at places where we think the old town plan intersects with, and occasionally contradicts, the modern city grid. One day a column in Argos on Corn Market, the next, a staircase in the Linen Hall Library.

Our thesis is that, even when all physical trace is gone, walls persist. Not altogether original, you might say, but in Belfast, where peace walls remain an all too visible fact, it is pertinent to Declan's mind and mine. Our hope is that we can collaborate with an architectural institute in Berlin. Not altogether surprising, you might also say, but Berlin is a city to which we both feel bound by something more than bricks and mortar.

On my own first trip to Berlin, in the spring of 1990, I paid a visit to the Reichstag, whose rear wall was just feet from the other wall – the Berliner Mauer – and whose sole purpose seemed to be the housing of a 'permanent' exhibition, *Fragen an die Deutsche Geschichte* (Questions on German History). The sixth of its seven rooms covered the period of the Third Reich, and there I encountered a photograph that showed a man kneeling, a soldier behind him with a pistol, and a crowd of onlookers. It was clear what was about to happen, yet the expression on the victim's face was not one of terror, but rather of disgust that this thing was being done to him, that these people were capable not just of doing it, but of watching it being done.

I say I encountered this photograph. Actually, I was stricken before it.

Long after I had returned home, I was turning over the components in my head – the victim, the executioner, the audience – haunted by the thought that, as much as I wanted to imagine I could only ever find myself in the place of the kneeling man, there was nothing in my DNA, my Glenn Patterson-ness, that absolutely guaranteed I could not end up playing either of the other roles. The only safeguard that I could see was vigilance against any ideology that reduced human beings to the one word for which they could be murdered (Jew, Commie, Prod, Taig, Brit, Mick ... or fascist, come to that); and against yourself, that you didn't just shrug such language off. By the time the onlookers have gathered, the victim has been made to kneel and the soldier is pointing his gun, it is far too late to ask how you got here.

It became such a mantra that I cited the photo repeatedly over the years. Always I talked of the near-uniform age of all those depicted, and always I talked about the expression on the victim's face as he looked at those looking at him about to be shot. I would sometimes talk too about the intimacy of mass murder: how it was far from unusual for the victims to be known to their killers, or to those who aided and abetted them.

Eventually I began to think there was a book there I should write: identify as many of the people in the photograph as possible, work back from that moment of the shot about to be fired, see how they all arrived at that lethal configuration. I wrote to a friend in Berlin, describing the photograph and its significance to me and asking if she knew what had become of the Questions on German History exhibition once the Reichstag had got its Fostered glass dome and become the Bundestag. My friend wrote back that the exhibition had been broken up and the images dispersed to the various libraries and collections from which they had been drawn. In fact, she had already spoken to people in two of the most important archives in Berlin. Neither held the photograph I was after, but it was early days and she would keep looking. A couple of weeks later I had another email. She had now been in touch with all the archives. Not only had she not found the photograph, she had not found anyone who thought her description of it sounded at all familiar.

'There are not many photographs,' she wrote, 'with just one guy being shot.'

She sent me a scan of the only one she had turned up. I opened the attachment and closed it almost instantly. It was totally wrong: for a start, the victim was not facing his audience, who in turn were not baiting him. Most tellingly of all, the execution was taking place on the edge of a mass grave, whereas I had specifically described a city street.

25

An hour or two later I opened the attachment again. There was certainly something familiar in the cast of the victim's eyes. I was looking at a scan of a copy of the original, but the expression was definitely not one of terror. The casual stance of the soldier with the gun was not unfamiliar either. And though the onlookers were not as gleeful as I had remembered (and were also to a man, soldiers, not civilians), there was something disturbing in the simple fact of their looking on, even in one case leaning to the side to see around a comrade who had cut across the sightlines.

For the first time it occurred to me that with the passing of years I might have tidied up the image that had so paralysed me when I first saw it in the Reichstag, and made it more neatly allegorical, geometrical, even: a triangle of morality.

It is in many ways more appalling than I had remembered, as is the legend – in the hand of a German soldier – on the back: 'The last Jew in Vinnitsa'. I realize that my search for it must seem incredibly dated now: today I could, if I wanted to, click on any one of several thousand websites and view that and other atrocity photographs that survive from that time. It might surprise some people that so few do; although that's another thing that has changed, since the Second World War, certainly, but even in the last decade. Where once perpetrators went to enormous lengths to cover up their massacres and atrocities, now they post them online.

The Vinnitsa photo came to represent something else, too – a reminder of how warily you must tread when you try to enlist the past, however good your intentions, and indeed however modest your enterprise.

Maybe that is one of the reasons Declan Hill and I have proceeded so slowly with our map: we are pretty sure we are on to something, but we are reluctant to force the issue, to see what we want to see rather than what we can.

Every so often, though, in large ways and small, standing before a photograph in the Reichstag, or looking down at an inexplicable kink in the staircase of the Linen Hall, history seems to buttonhole you and ask, 'Have you seen? Have you understood?' And then, 'What are you going to do about it?'

Guardian, 25 October 2014

Hives

Under the old Stormont regime, Ulster had hives. They were the official rash of the Unionist Party and like the Unionist Party, brooked no opposition. No one knew what caused hives exactly, beyond an excess of orange. With the imposition of Direct Rule in March 1972, hives were abolished and allergies introduced. (Orange was abolished too and juice gradually phased in.) I was called to the City Hospital for an allergy test shortly after Stormont was prorogued. I went behind a curtain and rolled up my sleeve. A doctor came in and laid a grid over my arm and pricked each space with a needle dipped in a different solution. Then he went behind the next curtain and the next and the next. By the time he returned to me two red lumps had risen up on my arm. 'House dust and school dust,' he said delightedly. They itched like mad, but I was as glad to see them as he was. I had been imagining a bigger grid next time, even more solutions and needle pricks – a million and a half of them maybe – until we came up with the reaction that was uniquely mine.

It was a lot more democratic than hives, but a lot more labour intensive too. Eventually the authorities stopped testing and started broadcasting, inventing Radio Ulster in 1975. (Don't ask me why Downtown Radio was invented, or what the fuck Cool FM is for.) I have lost count of the things I found out I might be allergic to thanks to the Radio Ulster weekend schedule, the things I have given up as a result, although I am admittedly in the giving up phase of my life. (The only thing I've *taken* up since I was thirty is flossing. I still drink, unlike a friend who finally discovered she had an allergy to alcohol: it made her do crazy things.)

For years many people here believed that it was only thoughts of the Other Sort that made them break out, but a recent survey showed that religion is not the sole irritant: twenty-five per cent of people in Northern Ireland are in fact allergic to people of a different race or sexual orientation living beside them.

We didn't know back in the days of concentrated orange, but really hives were the very least of what ailed us.

Vacuum, March 2007

Dal

Sometime in the summer of 1989 I started to come a bit unhinged. I had moved out of the house I shared with my girlfriend in England and returned to Belfast to write my second novel. Or perhaps more accurately, to worry about not writing my second novel, about the prospect of never writing another novel again, and about my lifestyle generally.

I had already stopped smoking – scrunched up an almost-full box of Marlboro Lights one afternoon and threw it across the room. It missed the bin, but I left it anyway, where it landed, as an added goad. I was keeping an eye on my drinking – an occasionally blurry eye – but keeping an eye nonetheless. People didn't speak the language of units then, but I wrote down in my diary each morning what I had drunk the night before, just as I had once written down how many fags I had smoked.

One August Saturday I woke and thought I had to stop eating meat. Just like that. There had, I seem to recall, been a television exposé earlier in the week about conditions on a battery farm, which had literally put me off my dinner; but the decision was not ethical. I just felt I had to do something more, something that would make it possible, or allow me to convince myself that it was possible (for somewhere not very far back that was what this was all about) to finish this fucking novel.

As I say, unhinged.

The first thing I did was empty my fridge and kitchen cupboards and pile all the food on the table. If I was going to be a vegetarian I was going to have to think like a vegetarian, not just leave a meat-shaped hole on my plate. Anything that looked as if it was waiting for a couple of sausages or a half-pound of mince to make its life complete went in the bin.

That done, I caught the train into town, walked from the station to Waterstone's and went straight to the cookery section. I made my choice according to width: I wanted the book with the most recipes. Rose Elliot's *Complete Vegetarian Cookbook* won by a good half-inch. I took it with me to the only wholefood shop in central Belfast and set about restocking my cupboard. I brought home a lot of lentils.

I was already a fan of Indian food from my time living in England: chicken curries, prawn curries, on a rare occasion, lamb curries. I hadn't, that I could remember, until that day eaten a lentil curry, or dal. (The spelling toggles between 'dal' and 'dhal'.) There were two recipes in the Rose Elliot book. I picked the second one on the strength of the sentence that read, 'this makes a hotter-tasting dal than the previous recipe'.

My spices had survived the cupboard cull. I even had some of the creamed coconut this particular recipe called for. (I have never since eaten another dal that did.) It did not call for a boiled egg quartered on top, but I added one anyway – I was turning vegetarian, not vegan. Barely half an hour after starting to cook, I sat down to eat.

It was so good I almost cried. I could live like this, no hardship. This wasn't a giving up, like smoking: this was an embracing. Also, it had cost about 50p.

I ate it again the next night and the night after that. I ate it, I would hazard, at least twice a week from then until I finished the novel, two years later, and went back to England. Actually, I would hazard I've rarely gone more than a week without dal in the almost quarter of a century since. There have been variations — many, many variations, for the ways with dal and its possible pulses are legion. I feel bound to try every new recipe I come across. My current favourites are a *panchmael* (five-lentil) dal, a *toor* — or *toovar* — dal from Bangladesh, soured with tomatoes and tamarind water, and a Nepalese version made exclusively with hulled mung beans. Touted by the British food writer Felicity Cloake as 'perfect', it's not far off.

But still sometimes I go back to that first Rose Elliot recipe. (The book doesn't fall open at page 191: it jumps.) Because in a way that sounds ridiculous now, but made complete sense at the time, it saved me.

The Economist Intelligent Life magazine,
March/April 2014

Twelfthish

From time to time I write a blog for the *Guardian* newspaper's online edition. Ten days ago, I attempted to post my, and perhaps the *Guardian's*, shortest-ever blog. Under the heading *Céad Míle Quid*, it said simply, 'Orangefest? O, Brethren'. When the editor suggested that I add a little more, for the benefit of the non-Northern Irish readership, not to say my future blogging career, I declined. It was all in those six words, I said: the £100,000 awarded to the Orange Order to re-brand the Twelfth, my scepticism about the name, about the whole attempt to turn the day into a major tourist attraction. There was nothing more to say.

That was before I was called by a reporter at Radio 4 who had somehow picked up (so the paper-cup-and-string survives into the era of blogs, I thought unkindly) that there is a crisis of identity in the unionist-voting community, or, more particularly, in the ever-larger community of Protestants who can't even be bothered going to the polls anymore. The way he saw it, Orangefest was less a sop to the marching orders and

33

their potentially disruptive supporters (let's just say Whiterock, 2005) than a symptom of this identity crisis: look at us! Love us! We're not scary! Heck, we even have stilt-walkers.

That, in turn, was before a judge found that two Liverpool men had been using Orange lodges as a cover for their UVF activities, before news broke that an Eleventh Night bonfire in Derry was displaying furniture stolen from a Polish man, who had fled his home a few days earlier after being stabbed in the leg.

Identity crisis? Full-blown schizophrenia, more like.

Yet even as I write that I wonder if it isn't a cheap shot. (For a start the Orange Order has no control over the bonfires, even if one of the ambitions of Orangefest is to take some of the heat out of the Eleventh Night too.) Perhaps my contact at Radio 4 does have a point and the Orange Order is attempting a manoeuvre every bit as tricky as the one the republican movement has been trying for a decade and more to execute (sorry, republican movement, I know how sensitive you are to the 'e' word just now) only with tens of thousands more members to try, not always successfully, to keep in step. If it can't change where it is marching from, historically speaking – all those Dolly's Braes and Drumcrees – then perhaps the Orange can change where it is marching to.

My own attitude to the Twelfth has gone from adolescent enthusiasm (stilt-walking is nothing when you have staggered along beside your favourite band in a pair of platforms, still suffering from the bonfire-night before), through twenty years of absolute hostility, to my present something-like indifference. The Universal Declaration of Human Rights guarantees me many things, but the right never to see and hear things I disagree with is not among them.

Actually, I like to think I was ahead of the game in dreaming up ways to sell the Twelfth overseas. Watching the 1990 Belfast demonstration for an article I was writing on the Battle of the Boyne's tercentenary I had a brainwave: twin the Twelfth with San Francisco's Gay Pride Parade. Where else outside of San Francisco, I asked myself, would you see so many chunky black moustaches and tight satin pants? Think of the new spirit of toleration that would be born in Northern Ireland, the interesting new beats introduced to America's West Coast.

But times, uniforms, and tastes in facial hair – even in Northern Ireland – change. So here (because I am sure in this new era the Grand Master reads the *Irish Times*) are a few suggestions for how the Orange Order might set about its twenty-first century makeover.

(1) Send a delegation to the Ukraine, see what an Orange majority really looks like, what it has to say about democracy in 2006.*

(2) Get in touch with your phone-company namesake and arrange for the John Tavener music used in its 2002 ad campaign to be distributed to all flute bands. It'd be a welcome break from 'Derry's Walls' and 'The Dambusters'.

(3) Agree to hold the parade on the Saturday nearest 12 July and rename it the Twelfth-ish. You would be amazed at the humility that comes with the addition of those three letters, amazed too at the gratitude of people not forced to take a public holiday for an event that celebrates something they feel no affinity with.

(4) Should you do nothing else, expel from your ranks forthwith any members found to have connections to paramilitary organisations and refuse to hire any band that glorifies by name or image the activities of those organisations.

* Oops.

I don't expect that even then they will be queuing up to strew your path with petals in parts of Belfast, but at least they might take at face value your protestation that you are in essence a religious body.

To people on the rest of the island, meanwhile, I would say, suspend your disbelief, come and have a look. You might oppose everything that the Order stands for, but, assuming (4) above is enacted, I find it hard to imagine that you would be offended by what you see. Mind you, I find it just as hard to imagine that having seen it once you would want to come back and see it again. In between the bands and the banners – and the Orangefest add-ons – are the lodges, mile upon mile of them. And, with membership dropping, they are not getting any younger.

Don't be fooled by the colourful name, or by the more colourful denunciations; unless you are already one of the converted, Orangeism on the march can be a pretty grey affair.

The Irish Times, 10 July 2006

An Encounter

People say to me, 'You must meet some right characters.' 'Not as many as I'd like,' I want to say, then remember the man I met on the Luas from Connolly Station to Heuston, the time I went to Limerick for the Kate O'Brien Weekend.

Upper fifties, I would have said.

I thought, when I saw him get on at Abbey Street, of a class of career messenger that the internet and the mountain-bike boys had all but swept from our city streets. The shine on the shoes, the exactness of the creases in his suit trousers, was a rebuke to most of today's bank *managers*.

It was that hour between the extended end of lunch and the start of the Friday night flight to the suburbs; he could have had any seat he wanted. He chose the seat facing me. I had an A4 notebook open on my lap at the page where, as the Enterprise pulled out of Belfast Central, two hours before, I had written the title of my paper – 'The State of Us' – and then nothing more; he carried a leather zip-folder from which he withdrew a Replacement Passport application form. He held it at arm's length a few moments, without focusing on it at all. Instead he looked at me. I nodded, went back to my notebook, and, more to be seen to be too busy to talk, added a colon after 'Us', and the subtitle 'How the North Wrote Itself into a Corner'.

'That's great what you're doing there,' he said.

'Sorry?'

'You sit there turning the thoughts over then' – he described the action in the air – 'you write the thing down. I couldn't do that.'

The Replacement Passport form was back in the folder.

'It's how I think best,' I said and for a quarter of a minute while we waited for a light to cross O'Connell Street he left me staring at the page, thoughtless.

'I have all the words in the world up here.' He pointed to his forehead and right enough it was as broad and flat as a dictionary. 'But put a piece of paper in front of me ...' His fingers grasped at something elusive.

He's telling me he can't write, I thought, or read. He could talk, though. I imagined arriving at Heuston and discovering he was on the Limerick train too. I imagined arriving in Limerick with my paper unwritten. I dropped my eyes, hoping to short-circuit the conversation. He allowed me fewer than fifteen seconds this time. 'Right, so.' His hand cut across the space between us, as straight as a ploughshare. I had no option but to grasp it.

'This is how we shake hands in my country, the hand coming in strong and direct,' he said.

Which in more ways than one put me in my place.

At Jervis Street the carriage filled with shopping bags. Arnotts, Debenhams, M&S, Next. A woman plumped into the seat beside me, a man, face a match for hers in tan, into the one next to the messenger, who asked him outright where he was from.

'Malta.' said the man, taking in his interrogator's appearance; if he had been asked for his bank account details he would have given them too.

He and his wife, he said, without waiting to be asked, were celebrating their twenty-fifth wedding anniversary. They had always wanted to come to Ireland.

The messenger stayed him with a raised forefinger.

'The full name of my country, with respect, is Eire,' he said and because I knew he couldn't read it I wrote the sentence down. I wrote down the whole conversation.

'Eire,' the Maltese couple repeated.

The messenger pointed again to his forehead. 'I have a large knowledge of my language.'

One half of the brain for Irish, I thought, one half for English.

He asked the couple where else they had been: Mayo, they said, and he approved; asked them if they had been enjoying his music, his Gaelic football; his hurling.

Four Courts, Smithfield, Museum; the Luas closed in on Heuston Station. The messenger continued to hold forth.

'My people are known as a nation of sellers: cattle and potatoes, going back to my father's time, 1922.' He was that specific: twenty-two. 'You didn't need to write anything in the market square.'

He's winding up for the ploughshare again, I thought, and sure enough, out went the arm, strong and direct, wife first, husband second.

He leaned in as he shook. 'Hand in hand, eye in eye, that's how we do things here.'

The tram stopped and the doors opened. Heuston.

'The world has changed terribly in recent years,' he said, from the corner of his mouth furthest from me. 'Too many false people.'

He means me, I thought, and wrote it down regardless.

Sunday Miscellany, RTÉ I, August 2009

Niall and Rory

Last weekend was a pretty good weekend to be young in Belfast. On Saturday the city's new Lord Mayor, Niall Ó Donnghaile of Sinn Féin, hosted his first Lord Mayor's parade. Mr Ó Donnghaile is twenty-five, the youngest person to hold the office in Belfast's four-hundred-year history.

On Sunday, Rory McIlroy, three years the Lord Mayor's junior, became the youngest winner of the US Open since 1924.

I have no interest in golf. The victory of another Northern Irishman, Graeme McDowell, in last year's US Open more or less passed me by. I have, though, an interest in narrative, and Rory McIlroy's progress to the first of his Majors (for there will be many more) has, in simple story terms, been compelling. His father, who worked long hours as a barman at the Holywood Golf Club where Rory started to play, placed a bet seven years ago that his teenage son would win the British Open by 2014. (He got odds of 500:1, odds that after events at Congressional no sane bookmaker on earth would offer.) Then there was that dramatic collapse on the final day of the Masters back in April. McIlroy sounded to me then utterly convincing when he said he would learn from the experience. He did not sound to me as though it was the end of his world. But that's being young for you: there will be other opportunities.

Niall Ó Donnghaile has already seized the opportunity of his first days as Lord Mayor to visit the Protestant Shankill Road, a significant gesture for a Sinn Féin politician. His appointment (the mayor here is not directly elected but nominated by the victorious party in local elections) was criticised by some who complained that he wouldn't know how things worked in our City Hall. 'Brilliant', wrote one commentator, not renowned for her sympathy with Sinn Féin: finally we might have a leader who was not weighed down by the 'excess baggage' of the past.

Ó Donnghaile's electoral ward is Pottinger on the east bank of the River Lagan from Belfast city centre and at the start of the road that five miles further on arrives in Holywood. I am, geographically speaking, somewhere in between. Chronologically I am Ó Donnghaile's age and McIlroy's combined, and then a few.

I didn't go so far as to watch the Open – it is still golf, a game played by men in slacks – but I did follow Sunday's final round online, shot by shot, until it seemed mathematically impossible for an implosion of Masters' proportions to reoccur.

The overnight victory was the lead story on every news bulletin here on Monday morning. It was the lead story on every lunchtime bulletin and all the talk on radio programmes in between. The tourism minister was interviewed about the possible effects on 'golf tourism', what with our previous staple 'Troubles tourism' apparently in decline, and with the *Titanic* centenary extravaganza another year away.

I had stopped listening to the news by the time, in the late evening, the story changed to the more familiar one of rioters on the streets of east Belfast, specifically around that part of the Pottinger Ward where the Protestant Newtownards Road runs up against the Catholic Short Strand. (We still, alas, refer to districts as Protestant and Catholic.) The first I knew of the trouble was waking in the early hours to the sound of police helicopters. In my confusion I thought it might be a US Open winner being escorted home. It was my wife who reminded me that we had seen people bolting metal grilles to the windows of houses along the Short Strand 'interface' as we drove from town earlier in the evening. The implication that the violence was not the spontaneous outburst of what are usually referred to as 'community tensions' was borne out by the police, who laid the blame at the door of the UVF (Ulster Volunteer Force). The UVF came into existence around the time that the *Titanic* was being launched and re-emerged in the 1960s as the most deadly of the several Protestant terrorist organisations. Like all the others, the UVF was supposed to have 'left the stage' some time ago.

A mural celebrating the building of the *Titanic* can be seen in the background of many of the photographs of the rioting that began on Monday night and continued into Tuesday: east Belfast is the home of the famous Harland and Wolff shipyard. The rioters in the foreground are mostly masked, but many appear to be considerably younger than even Rory McIlroy, younger, some of them, than our seventeen-year-old Peace Process, although as I never tire of saying, anything *that* processed can't have a lot of good left in it.

Rory McIlroy himself finally flew into George Best Belfast City Airport on Tuesday evening. (The airport is named for another of the city's – and the east's – sporting greats, the prodigiously talented, but fatally flawed star of Manchester

43

United and several MLS clubs.) In the photographs of him standing on the tarmac with the Open trophy you can glimpse the Harland and Wolff cranes.

As so often in Northern Ireland it all depends on how you look at it.

To Rory McIlroy this is the 'best place in the world', which a cynic might say is the kind of thing you can afford to think when you spend half your life away. A recent survey (Northern Ireland Life and Trends), however, seems to suggest that increasing numbers share his fondness for it, with over 50% of Catholics now in favour of a Northern Ireland within the United Kingdom over political reunification with the rest of Ireland. Sinn Féin disputes the findings, but for what it's worth, and despite this week's riots, my money is on the further development of a shared sense of Northern Irishness, symbolised by the likes of Rory McIlroy and by Niall Ó Donnghaile's visit to the Shankill. And on Rory winning the British Open, of course. Just not, sadly, at 500:1.

Bloomberg View, 22 June 2011

So Anyway

So anyway, it is the thirteenth anniversary of Ali's moving to Belfast, and Hallmark for some inexplicable reason not having a happy-anniversary-of-your-moving-to-Belfast section (yet, I suppose I should say: yet), we decide to go out for dinner to the same Indian restaurant we went to on the night in 1994 that Ali arrived here. Then it was a short walk from our front door, now it is a cab across town, although our driver approves of our destination ... or seems to approve. 'That's a great place, whatever the *Telegraph* says. After all, Michael Deane eats there and he knows a thing or two about kitchens.' It is only as we approach the restaurant door that I realize what he was talking about. (OK, so we don't get out that much any more, even with the anniversary of our meeting, and the anniversary of my proposing, which coincidentally is also the anniversary of my rendering myself unconscious in a Dublin restaurant not having noticed the warning on the way out to the toilets: 'Mind Your Head'.) So anyway, walking towards the door, I see the sign with the Food Standards Agency rating: No Stars. 'A general failure,' I read later, 'to comply with legal requirements. Little or no appreciation of food safety. Major effort is required.'

We are in a quandary. This is our anniversary. One of them. It is, because it is summer after all, pouring, and our taxi is already halfway down the road again into town. And it is midweek; we are tired; we have a small blonde alarm clock that is inclined to go off very, very early. We opt to stay, telling ourselves that if the taxi driver hadn't spoken, if we had not noticed the scores on the door, or if we had been here a couple of weeks earlier we would have been none the wiser.

The problem is that being the wiser it is hard to play dumber. We cover up for a while trying to remember exactly what we ate that night thirteen years ago, although knowing us back then, how thirsty we were, we would probably have been hard pressed to remember it the morning after. We order in the end what the people we have become think the people we were would have liked. The staff, it has to be said, could not be nicer: 'Thirteen years tonight! Imagine.' But it is no good. The food arrives, we eat, and it all tastes a bit, well, no-starry.

So, anyway, not one of our more memorable meals in the last thirteen years (possibly not even in our top five hundred), but an overdue introduction to one of the new realities of going out in Belfast. I am introduced to another, even more belatedly, a week or so later when I do something else I haven't done for a while and go for a drink with friends on a Saturday night.

The clouds have paused for refueling, so of course every available inch of footpath in front of every bar we try is jammed with people smoking. I'll admit at first it is all a bit disorienting – didn't we used to step *out of* the bar to get a breath of fresh air? – but very quickly I begin to see the health benefits. I'm not talking passive smoking, here; I'm talking active kicking. Time was you had to walk right into a place, maybe even go to the trouble and the expense of buying yourself a drink, before you realized that a sizeable part of the clientele didn't like the cut of your jib, in fact would quite happily cut you a new one.

Now pretty much everyone you would not care to meet is there on display on the footpath. Even when the rain returns (as return it must), the worst of them, you can guarantee, will be huddled under those little awnings that seem to have been bought in a job lot from the kind of hair salon your granny went to in the mid-1960s.

Scores on the Doors; Tough Guys Outside. It's a whole new city these days. Roll on our twenty-sixth Ali-moving-to-Belfast anniversary, I say.

News Letter, July 2007

The C-word

Late last year the Paul Hamlyn Foundation held a seminar in Belfast's Ulster Museum, as part of the Foundation's Artworks initiative, which supports artists working in 'participatory settings', a term apparently arrived at after a good deal of discussion as an alternative to 'community', although it was on the subject of community that I was invited there to speak. I thought twice – actually three or four times – before saying yes. I have problems of my own with the C-word and how it's used in Northern Ireland in particular.

What I ended up saying, therefore, was personal, a sort of turning up of the volume on an ongoing interior monologue, but it was also professional in that it had regard to the use of language. Coincidentally, I once heard the broadcaster Gerry Anderson in the same venue demolish in his usual, deceptively casual, and very funny way, a well-known film set in Belfast on the strength – or maybe that should be the weakness – of the dialogue in its opening scene: 'If the language is wrong,' he said, 'everything is wrong.'

The line has become something of a mantra for me, and on the basis of everything being wrong if the language is wrong, what I said to the seminar was also, I suppose, political.

The only way I know to approach anything is to ask questions. Here's my first one: how did it come to this? How did a word that has its roots in commonality end up one of the most vexed — and vexing — in our lexicon?

Here is another question: what is the difference between a 'community worker', a 'community practitioner', a 'community activist' and a 'community gatekeeper'? I recently worked on a radio documentary, about the Arts Council of Northern Ireland's attempts to 're-image' paramilitary murals, in the course of which I heard all those terms.

I think I understand the various shades of meaning contained within them. I think most people in Northern Ireland do too. I think we turn a blind eye, or at best raise a sardonic eyebrow, to what in certain instances the word community connotes.

My friend, and fellow writer, Colin Carberry, went to a primary school whose yard wall formed part of the Springfield Road peace line. He had a very apt — very Belfast — word for everything that lay on the other side: *Narnia*. When it comes to community, however, the sensation is rather of having passed Through the Looking Glass: 'When *I* use a word,' Humpty Dumpty said, in a rather scornful tone, 'it means just what I choose it to mean — neither more, nor less.' 'The question is,' said Alice, 'whether you *can* make words mean so many different things.' 'The question is,' said Humpty Dumpty (who sounds as though he has rung in to Stephen Nolan), 'which is to be master — that's all.'

I have been ransacking my brain and I think the first time I heard the word community — outside perhaps of the Monopoly board – was in the name Community Relations Commission, a forerunner of the present Community Relations Council, which was formed in the final months of 1969 by the Community Relations (Northern Ireland) Act.

(I was eight, but the events of the previous summer had already made a news and current affairs veteran of me.)

Employing one of my foremost writer's skills – counting words – I can tell you that 'community' appears twenty-one times in the text of that act, fully twenty of them yoked to its partner 'relations', and even the one remaining usage – 'harmonious relations throughout the community' – could be described as an instance of elegant variation, although it is worth dwelling for a moment on that particular phrase, 'relations throughout *the* community …'

Compare that to another, more recent text, a widely praised speech to last month's British–Irish Parliamentary Assembly by Judith Gillespie, Deputy Chief Constable of the PSNI, in which she reported on changes in policing in the fifteen years since the signing of the Good Friday Agreement. Here again, would you believe, the word community occurs twenty-one times (I tell you, I could count words all day long) – more than any other word bar policing itself.

Actually, that is not strictly accurate: the word community appears twelve times; the plural – communities – entirely absent from the Community Relations Act, appears nine.

It is in the slippage from singular to plural that I think some of my problems with the C-word, or words, lie: community is a word of aggregation, communities is a word that, rather than multiplying, as most plurals do, actually divides.

Again, I think I understand the reasoning behind this change in number. In order to take some of the sectarian heat out of the political situation here, which the mild reforms and initiatives of late 1969 failed to improve, the labels Catholic and Protestant were first diluted by the addition of 'community' and then effaced almost completely as the Protestant and Catholic Communities became just the Two Communities.

But here is the curious thing: as soon as the Two Communities model was established the singular form itself was altered; it became the fragment rather than the thing greater than the sum of its parts.

The word has been pulled this way and that ever since, its uses and potential abuses proliferating, its every new appearance more surprising than the one before.

One of the most recent arrivals on the C-word scene is the Protestant Unionist Loyalist community, or PUL, a giant golf umbrella of a term: a GustBuster Pro Series Gold 62-incher, say, or even a DeLuxe Black Windproof 64-inch Arc Auto. (The things you find on the Internet.)

Now I am old enough that when I see a capital P and a capital L the vowel I automatically imagine sandwiched between them is not a U, but an l, as in *PiL*, Public Image Limited, the group that John Lydon formed when he quit the Sex Pistols and stopped being Rotten, and in fact at times during the past year – its flag disputes and Twelfth of July riots – I have watched some of what has been done in the name of the PUL community and have had to fight hard to banish the thought of it being played out against a soundtrack of PiL's 'Public Image', Lydon's outraged opening line, 'You never listened to a word that I said …'

Although that oft-repeated complaint – no one is listening to us – leads on to another question: how and through whom do communities speak?

I have got into the habit of saying that for the purposes of expressing our opinions on a whole range of issues in this country we are divided into constituencies and wards; but, like everyone else lately I have been following Russell Brand's lambasting of our electoral system, which in his words only ever delivers the equivalent of a hop to the left or a hop to the right, and, whichever direction the hop, is in the service finally of corporations and financial institutions, and for the first time in my adult life I have wondered about the wisdom of voting.

I suspect I am not alone in Northern Ireland in never having found a political party here that I could vote for with enthusiasm, or even one that I much liked. Only once, voting for the party I dislike least, have I ended up being in the majority. Mostly I tell myself that I have to vote to be numbered among those who did not choose the inevitable victor, as a reminder that it is incumbent on that victor to represent *all of us*, irrespective of where we put our Xs or our 1-2-3s.

In that radio documentary I mentioned earlier I heard it said on numerous occasions that murals were not imposed on communities but came from them. Yet travelling around my city I was struck by the fact that they had a tendency to come from a *particular* angle. The suspicion remains that while community talks big – often very, very big – it defines a whole lot smaller, that in practice 'All of us' as often as not means, 'All of us who think like us.'

There was, for instance, in West Belfast not a mural quite, but a painted billboard that explicitly attacked Sinn Féin's main rival for nationalist votes, the SDLP, which is fair enough, you might say – all political parties are fair game – but you would hope that such attacks would come with a right of reply in the same medium. The SDLP currently accounts for 13.5 per cent of the vote in west Belfast. It actually gained a seat from Sinn Féin in the 2011 Belfast City Council election. In other words, while far from being the force that it once was, the SDLP is not without its supporters. If all the voices in that geographically defined community carried equal weight, then might you not expect, say, one mural in every nine or ten to reflect a more Social Democratic point of view?

As for murals elsewhere in the city, the current most conspicuous muralists are the UVF, whose members number a few hundred and whose closest aligned political party currently holds two of the fifty-one seats on Belfast City Council, in fact two of the seven hundred and eleven contestable seats across local government, Assembly, Westminster and European elections. It hardly seems a mandate for painting yet more gunmen over a mural of George Best. Unless of course this is an example of the bypassing of the electoral system Russell Brand has been advocating (in which case, Russell, be careful what you wish for), or unless indeed these things work the way the Censorship Board of Ireland used to work.

A couple of years ago I had the great good fortune to interview Edna O'Brien and was surprised to hear her make light of the banning of her first novel, *The Country Girls*: all it took in those days, she said, was half a dozen people complaining to the Bishop.

What are the critical numbers in Northern Ireland today? How many complaints to the brigadier does it take to get a fifteen-year-old boy (as a fifteen-year-old boy was this week) kneecapped?

On the subject of murals, by the way, when the UDA formed in the 1970s they were nicknamed the Wombles, I can only imagine because of the bush hats they wore, which resembled the one sported by the slothful Orinoco in the children's TV series. (And if ever there was a Womble destined for a drinking den it was Orinoco.)

In my Banksy fantasies I think to myself *that* would be a mural: hooded Wombles brandishing weapons.

Actually, what I would love to see, given that it is now being filmed in our midst, its cast practically a community, with as many members, from what I have seen of the series, as the UVF, are some *Game of Thrones* related murals and graffiti: 'You Are Now Entering the Free Cities'; 'The only good Stark is a dead

Stark'; and not forgetting of course (for the re-imaging stage) Greyjoy cultural icons.

This would have to be a two-way process. We would give them wall space and they would give us two places on the writing team. Shortly after which we could expect the appearance in the script of a special envoy, who, an episode or two later, would broker a seven-way power-sharing deal. Westeros would rise to number 8 on the Condé-Nast list of weekend break destinations, even allowing for tension around a few emotive dates, the Red Wedding anniversary chief among them.

It would be a lot less dramatic, *but*, in being transformed from a series to a *process*, it would never, ever end.

Back in the real world (*sic*) of Orange civil rights camps and concerned residents groups and pop-up peace lines, our own process has consolidated the Two Communities model. The checks and safeguards written into our aforementioned Big Agreement – which I voted for and would vote for again in the absence of anything better – those checks, those safeguards, with their language of mutual respect, though again proceeding from laudable intentions, have encouraged a particular form of active complacency, if that is not too much of an oxymoron, whereby at least as much energy – I would contend more – is expended on vigilance against criticism or perceived slight as on genuine self-reflection.

I still like the critic Edna Longley's line from back around the time of the Agreement that a bit more parity of *dis*esteem would not have gone amiss.

Stretching yourself means more than reaching out to 'the other side'.

I can't help thinking, for instance, that one of the greatest institutions in our city, two hundred and twenty-five years old this year, was founded as the Belfast Library and Society for *Promoting Knowledge*. Out of this Linen Hall Library, as it came to be known, grew the Belfast Natural History and Philosophical Society, through whose efforts the city's first museum was built, by public subscription, 182 years ago. That museum became in time the Old Museum, which became the Old Museum Arts Centre, or OMAC, whose DNA, or M-A-C, is present in our own, newly opened Metropolitan Arts Centre (aka the MAC) on St Anne's Square.

There is implicit in the names of both those original societies a desire for self-, dare I say communal-, improvement. And lest anyone should think they were the inventions of some privileged elite, the founders of the reading society that grew into the Library were described by a contemporary as 'worthy plebeians' or '*sans-culottes*'. It's hard to think of an exact equivalent in today's idiom, especially since both have a note of condescension, but 'ordinary working people' comes close. People, I would guess, much like us, or much like we would like to imagine ourselves.

So what, it is worth asking, will the legacies of our own era be? What are we doing, or bringing into being, today that will continue to benefit the citizens of 2238?

Do we want to better ourselves or just *feel* better about ourselves?

This has particular relevance I think when it comes to the role of the arts and artists 'in participatory settings', although even writing those words does seem to suck just a little bit of the life out of what it is that all of us do when we sit down – or stand up – to work, about what so excited us when we embarked on our somewhat rickety career paths. (I am thinking, by the way, of running a class one of these days called All Those Things You Do That You Think Are Incidental To Your Career And Turn Out To Be The Career Itself.)

Almost twenty-five years ago the Arts Council of Northern Ireland appointed me Artist-in-the-Community for Lisburn and Craigavon. For two and a half years I organised readings, set up and judged short story competitions, and generally tried to promote writing in those two areas. I ran a writing group in Brownlow Library, I ran a group in Lurgan Library and I ran a group in Portadown Library, which, of the three of them, is the one that sticks in my head the most, and not just because of the somewhat nerve-racking walk from the Library to the train station for the last train home at a time when Portadown was wearing its least united-community face and when the train station functioned as a *de facto* peace line.

There was a man, Jimmy, who started coming to this group about halfway through my time there. I would guess he was then in his late sixties and he was in the most pleasant of ways a disruptive presence: a raker, a slagger, took nothing seriously, least of all himself. He would chuckle through our discussions of the extracts I brought in: 'Too deep for me,' he'd say, while his response to everything that the other members of the group wrote was the equivalent of an appreciative whistle, 'Boy's a dear, that's powerful.'

Every week I would ask him if he would not write something himself — for he was a great, almost incessant storyteller — to which the reply was always the same: 'Not at all, sure I wouldn't know how to write.'

'Exactly the way you speak,' I'd say, but no, not at all, not at all, he couldn't, wouldn't.

Until the very last meeting — the end of my two and a half years — when Jimmy surprised us all by pulling from his pocket a couple of handwritten pages, which amid great hilarity and with no little mock ceremony he proceeded to read ... And it was, if not the saddest story I have ever heard (Ford Madox Ford copyrighted that) then easily the saddest I have heard read in any writing group I have ever been involved with, anywhere.

Its central character was Jimmy himself, in his youth, in love with a girl he thought too good for him, whom he nevertheless found the courage or the front (I could believe that of him) to ask out. Some of the details of the story have slipped my mind in the intervening years, so I might be stretching it by saying he was going to ask her to marry him, but what I remember clearly is that one of his friends, happening to meet the girl in the street, told her he was glad to hear about her and Jimmy and was sure that in time Jimmy's other girlfriend would be glad too.

It was a joke, a bit of 'raking about', but the girl didn't know that, and Jimmy didn't know why she suddenly froze him out, until years later, when the friend owned up.

And this is the saddest bit: Jimmy never did find anybody else.

That explained everything to me. How could anyone take anything seriously after that?

Now I could not say whether Jimmy had been waiting all his life to tell that story, or whether out of sympathy for me – for that was the type of him: goodhearted – he had decided he would write something and that was the only story he had. I think I can say, however – and this is not to flatter myself – that he would not have written it at all if it had not been for that group.

And I have no idea how – if it had not been the last week – I could have told him what to do to make the story better. It was the unrepeatable event of his reading it that gave it its special power. I honestly believe that was enough for him. Of course in today's world where everything is recorded or uploaded or tweeted and re-tweeted such once-and-once-only occurrences are increasingly rare. There is as never before a pressure to publish. Which is the point at which the question of improvement becomes unavoidable. *Every* piece of writing can be made better.

Incidentally, I don't know how many community writing groups there are in Iceland, or for that matter how many in community activists, practitioners or gatekeepers. I do know, from an article in the BBC News Magazine of 13 October 2013, that a staggering one in ten of the country's population of 300,000 will publish a book in the course of their lives: fiction, non-fiction, poetry, children's . . .

Rosie Goldsmith, the author of the article, advances various reasons for this exceptional figure: the cataclysmic banking collapse of 2008, which hit Iceland early and hard, the volcanic ash cloud a couple of years later, either or both of which may have had the effect of throwing Icelanders back on their own resources.

She also mentions – and this seems to me as important a detail as ash clouds and banking collapses – that in the run-up to Christmas every house in Iceland gets a book catalogue through the door. Icelanders give books as presents, lots and lots of them.

Having acknowledged the usefulness of community writing groups – and let us be frank about this, the usefulness to artists trying to make a living as well as writing group members – I am bound to say that I still think the best writing courses are to be found on the fiction shelves and poetry shelves of any bookshop, and better yet, if you go into any library they are to be found absolutely free.

It doesn't have to have community in front of it to benefit the community. The word public used to serve us all very well.

A few days after that *News Review* article appeared the *Guardian* ran an interview with Barry McGuigan, now manager of Belfast fighter Carl Frampton, who until he vacated the titles last week was the European and Commonwealth super bantamweight champion. Talking about his own career in the ring, McGuigan said: 'For many of us boxing was a sanctuary. It was a release and an education. We travelled the world and met other people. And we became better human beings. Boxing was unique.'

I can't tell you how much this delighted me. Another person than Barry McGuigan might have been tempted to insert a couple of 'communities' there: 'For many of us the boxing *community* was a sanctuary ... The boxing *community* was unique.' We do that a lot here. We needlessly bulk out the sentence so that rather than gain clarity it loses definition, becomes flabby. We make adjectives out of nouns, make community the ever-present thing itself ... Like the presenter of Radio Ulster's *Evening Extra* programme, the night before my lecture, during an item on hands-free phones, referring to the *driving* community.

That is perhaps a bit of a cheap shot, cheap because the presenter was live on air and searching, by the sound of him, for a sheet of paper, and cheap because I write as someone who has expended a lot of ink in the past trying to refute the Two Communities model by arguing for recognition of the many other communities that exist – the Traveller community, the Gay and Lesbian community, the Polish community, the Chinese community, the Manchester United supporting community, the Anybody *but* United community, the community of those who want to tear their hair out when they have to fill in the box on the census that asks them what their perceived community is.

Enough already. Less ink, less flab: we need greater precision. To invoke Gerry Anderson again, we need to keep testing the language to ensure that it is right for the moment in which we find ourselves.

I recently got back from a trip to Canada in the course of which I helped my uncle and my cousin's husband change a set of car brakes, or rather in the course of which I stood in the presence – and occasionally, I am sure, irritatingly, right in the light – of my uncle and my cousin's husband while they changed the brakes. My uncle, working-class Belfast by birth, was, until he retired, a park warden in Ontario; my cousin's husband is an English lecturer – an English lecturer, he would be quick to add, from Regina in Saskatchewan, where, he said – although he thought it might apply more widely across Canada, or might once have – people took pride in being able to fix things themselves. My uncle's garage was as baffling to me as five aisles of B&Q, without the product descriptions, but it was my cousin's husband who brought most of the tools required for this task, along with handwritten instructions, although before I make this sound like an episode of *The Waltons*, I should add that when things got particularly tricky they had recourse to not one but two iPads and a mobile phone, which my cousin's husband used to phone his father – in Regina – the man by whom the handwritten instructions had been dictated.

Between them they jacked up the car, removed the lugs from the wheel, lifted the wheel off then took out the bolts holding the brake calliper in place, separated the calliper into its two constituent parts, one of which they attached by bungee rope to the undercarriage, while they set about removing the brake pads and finally the brake rotor.

I could go on at great length. I could go on, as my uncle and my cousin's husband went on, for three hours. What I did for those three hours, apart from talk, was marvel (I was reminded of a passage in Don DeLillo's *Underworld* in which an old priest tells the young central character a propos of the parts of a shoe, 'you didn't see the thing because you don't know how to look. And you don't know how to look because you don't know the names …'); talk, marvel, and occasionally pass a wire brush.

Part of the talk I maintained, indeed, was about all those wonderful lost job titles that you find in old censuses and street directories, of which I was sure Wire-Brush-Passer must be one.

Actually, I read another interview lately, with Paul McCartney, in which – the interviewer remarked – he seemed a little vague as to what Beatles tracks were on what albums, but he remembered very clearly his first-ever job, on leaving school, which was 'second man' in a van – that was the job title, Second Man – the 'first man' being the van driver.

The world has changed too completely for those trades and minutely demarcated job titles of Paul McCartney's youth to return – this part of the world has changed beyond all recognition and finally for the better – if not, yet, the best – since the authors of the 1969 Act attempted to regulate and improve relations between people here, but in the same way that euphemisms can in time become more offensive than the words they are intended to shield us from, so I think it is time we threw off the veils of our once protective communities, become nouns again if you like, personal pronouns even, and see if there isn't a more enabling way for us all to reconnect. There are enough dirty political words here, let's take the C-word back, keep that for very best.

Louis MacNeice is the author of what ought to be adopted as our national lyric – rather than national anthem – the poem 'Snow' – written in what used to be the residence of the Bishop of Down Connor (a position his father held) and is now the home of the Arts Council of Northern Ireland: 'World is suddener than we fancy it. World is crazier and' – these are the words at which we should all get to our feet and link hands – 'more of it than we think incorrigibly plural.'

Around the time that I received the invitation to speak at the Artworks seminar – the Monday after that business with the brakes, to be exact – I happened to be reading another of his poems, the book-length 'Autumn Journal', written in 1938, published in 1939. Come to think of it, it might have been because I was reading 'Autumn Journal' at that moment that I said yes, for which, I appreciate, you might never find it in you to forgive Louis MacNeice. But anyway, in Canto XII of the poem – the Journal's virtual midpoint – he writes:

'All that I would like is to be human, having a share/ In a civilized, articulate and well-adjusted/ Community where the mind is given its due/ But the body not mistrusted.'

To which I would add one final question: who wouldn't want to live in that Community?

A version of this piece appeared in *The Irish Times*, 4 January 2014

Names

Breakfast-time, mid August, the Second Summer of Rain. Our two-and-a-half-year-old is chewing something over; something more substantial than a bagel.

'So, sometimes you're Daddy, sometimes you're Glenn and sometimes you're Dad.'

'That's right.'

She chews some more. 'Well, I think I'm going to call you Dad.'

The six-year-old ('My Sister', as the younger has taken to calling her, as in 'what cereal is My Sister having this morning?') is concerned.

'That means I won't be able to call you Daddy either.'

She understands that the choice is not arbitrary, that there is a strict mathematics at work here, a precise ratio of syllables to age. Older ought to mean shorter. Already some of her school friends have subtracted the '-dy', and once gone it is hard to add it on again.

'Although,' she says, after a moment contemplating her bowl (Cheerios: Your Sister is having Cheerios), 'Sky Masterson is always talking about the things his daddy told him and Sky Masterson's probably in his thirties.'

Because it is mid August, the Second Summer of Rain, we have been watching a lot of musicals together lately: friends, in all innocence, of Dorothy, but also of Tony and Maria, their Jets and Sharks, of every orphan in the Hudson Street Home for Girls, and, as of yesterday, of the habitués of Nathan Detroit's Oldest Established Permanent Floating Crap Game in New York.

We have already had a long conversation about the 'dolls' in *Guys and Dolls* (derives, curiously enough from Dolly, a diminutive of Dorothy), and about the use of 'sister' and 'brother' at the Save a Soul Mission where Marlon Brando as Sky loses his heart to Jean Simmons's Sergeant Sarah Brown.

'That would be brothers and sisters in Christ, as in God the Father,' I told them – 'Or Daddy?' 'Not usually' – 'but you can also have brother- and sisterhood based on common interest, like in the French Revolution ...'

It really has been raining a lot this summer.

Back at the breakfast table, the younger says, 'Mum calls her Mum and Dad Em and Ger.'

'This is true.'

'You don't call yours Phares and Nessie,' her sister says.

'This is also true.'

It crosses my mind to tell them the story of my friend Thompy, back when we were teenagers, who having heard another of our friends call his parents by their first names went straight home and hailed his father, 'Right, Norman?' But the story ends with a severe smack around the head, which is not a conversation I want to start, not over the Cheerios, and especially not as all the rest of us did when Thompy told us was laugh. (We lived in a *Beano* world then, I sometimes think, of slippers and canes and thick ears. There were, in my own house, leather taws, the mere mention of which was guaranteed to send me into hysterics.)

'It's all a question of what comes naturally,' I say instead. 'Like, some people might find it odd me calling the two of you "bird".'

Their looks tell me that they find it odd anyone would find it odd.

Bird, it has to be said, is a relatively recent addition to my vocabulary. I believe – in so far as I have given it any thought beyond enjoying the sound of the word – that I am using it in its Middle English sense of maiden, or possibly even the Scots 'burd', meaning offspring. An American visitor to the house once commented on my previous term of endearment: 'lover'. Was it 'sweet' she called it, or 'quaint'? Whichever, I was never able to use it again without feeling self-conscious, although I had probably picked it up from my mum (definitely 'Mum'), who possibly knew that in Shakespeare it could be so un-freighted as to mean simply 'friend'.

My dad's mum – my Granny, as opposed to my mum's mum, my Gran – had a simple solution to all of this angst about terminology. Standing on her doorstep – for many years her chief occupation, aside from buying scones – she greeted all male passers-by with 'Hello, Man'; female with 'Hello, Woman'.

Which on reflection is perhaps not so far removed from a world composed entirely of guys and dolls.

But the bagel has been chewed, the Cheerios cheerioed. My wife – Mummy, Ali, Mum – is the musicals impresario today. I am off upstairs to work.

I stop at the kitchen door. 'I'll tell you what my old daddy used to say to me: "Call me anything you like, just don't call me back."'

I don't make it more than two steps down the hall.

'Back!' they chirp, delighted.

Sisters.

The Irish Times, August 2008

Poles Apart?

Aka 'Europe between Political Folklore and National Populism'

Queen Elizabeth I of England is reputed to have said that when she died the word 'Calais' would be found written on her heart. All I can say is that when I die I wouldn't be surprised if 'Europe' was found written on mine, followed in ever fainter script by the words that finished me off, 'between political folklore and national populism'. There were days at a time when I feared I would get up to deliver this lecture and have not a single thought in my head. There were still other days when I argued back and forth with myself whether the problem was my imagination or someone else's punctuation: 'Europe between political folklore and national populism'. I was muttering it at all hours of the day; I was starting to say it in my sleep.

In the end I decided to sit very still (I've been writing for twenty years, so I have plenty of practice) and let my mind wander down whatever paths of association the title led it. True, I was as likely to come up smelling of shit as I was smelling of roses, but at least it would be a definite smell; at least I wouldn't be left with my mouth hanging open, speechless.

*

I am not sure if you could call it 'political folklore' exactly, but the Irish novelist Colm Tóibín tells a very interesting story. (Sorry, the Irish novelist Colm Tóibín tells many very interesting stories. This one, however, to the best of my knowledge, has not yet appeared in one of his very interesting books.) On Sunday, 30 January 1972 – *Bloody* Sunday as it came to be known – British soldiers shot and killed fourteen unarmed civilians at a civil rights march in Derry, Northern Ireland's second city. Three days later a crowd of more than 20,000 marched on the British Embassy in Dublin's Merrion Square. Violence broke out; petrol bombs were thrown. An attempt was made to blow the embassy doors off their hinges. At the height of the protest Union Jacks were hung from the front of the building and set alight. The embassy was burnt to the ground.

That night – that historical moment – says Colm Tóibín, who was there, was pivotal, not just for him as an individual, but for all of Southern Irish society. There were only two options: you either followed through on the logic of the flames – threw yourself heart and soul into the conflagration that was raging across the border – or you let the embassy fire be an end point. Like the vast majority, Tóibín chose the latter option. In the aftermath of 2 February 1972, the Republic of Ireland, 'the South' in everyday speech, in the title of Colm Tóibín's own first novel (although it is partly set in Spain), the South turned its back on the North and in the same metaphoric motion turned its face towards Europe.

In January 1973 the Republic of Ireland joined the Common Market, as it was then. Northern Ireland, as an 'administrative region of the United Kingdom', to give it its correct title, joined at the same time. But while the South embraced Europe enthusiastically, the North continued to find less productive things to do with its arms. Northern Ireland, in fact, entered into a period of intense parochialism in which the sense of belonging was often limited to an area of a few square miles – sometimes considerably less. Belfast was so comprehensively divided that many people left 'their area' only to work, assuming, that is, they had work to leave for. The borders between these sectarian cantons were marked with flags and wall murals and, of course, with graffiti. One of the most common slogans in loyalist, or Protestant, working-class parts of town was 'No Pope Here': a reminder that in the very distant past the conflict that was consuming so much of our energy and economy – so many of our citizens' lives – had been part of a wider European religious war.

When in October 1978 Cardinal Karol Józef Wojtyla was named Pope John Paul II, the graffiti changed, in what passes with us for humour, to 'No *Pole* Here'. It was less a threat than a statement of fact. Even given the conditions prevailing in their own country in 1978, few Poles in their right minds would surely have dreamt of relocating to Belfast. Looking back almost thirty years at film footage of that time the city does have the air of a police state, where 'police' could be extended to cover those paramilitary organisations who held sway in loyalist and republican districts and who had their own very crude way of silencing oppositional voices: tape across the mouth, a hood over the head and a bullet in the nape of the neck.

Northern Ireland is famously a place where you cannot walk down a street without bumping into a poet, or at least cannot walk into a bar without bumping into one. Nothing any poet has written, however, comes as close to capturing the mood of those years for me as the words of a group of young men barely out of their teens: Belfast punk band Stiff Little Fingers, whose debut album, released four months after the 'No Pole Here' graffiti started to appear, contained a song called simply 'Here We Are Nowhere': *'Here we are nowhere, nowhere left to go.'*

Or as a friend of mine at the time used to say, 'Here we are floating in the Atlantic Ocean two-thirds of the way to the North Pole and we have the cheek to complain about the weather.'

'Nowhere', or 'near the North Pole', certainly could not have felt further removed from the rest of Europe: we didn't even seem to be made of the same stuff. What sticks in my memory most from my teenage years seeing news reports from Strasbourg and Brussels was the amount of glass in the buildings. In Belfast the window had given way to the security grille, the slit. Not only did we not feel part of Europe, we were in danger of losing sight of it entirely.

In the opening pages of his magnificent history of Europe, the British historian Norman Davies has a neat interpretation of the myth of Europa. Europa, if you remember your Ovid, was the mother of Minos, who while paddling in the surf of her native Phoenicia, that is to say today's southern Lebanon, encountered Zeus, in the guise of a snow-white bull. Europa allowed herself to be talked into clambering onto Zeus's back, whereupon the god whisked her across the waves to Crete. 'Zeus,' Davies writes, 'was surely transferring the fruits of the older Asian civilizations of the east to the new island colonies of the Aegean ... At the dawn of European history, the known world lay to the east. The unknown waited in the west.'

This is a reversal of almost all subsequent European history in which the 'centre' moved ever more steadily west (although sadly stopping well short of us in Belfast) and in which the east was increasingly characterised as a threat, wherever the east was deemed to begin at any given moment: the Bosporus Strait or the Brandenburg Gate. For the ultimate example of this westward drift I would suggest you look no further than Disneyland Paris. The Disney Corporation spent much time and money trying to locate the exact centre of Europe – deciding finally that it lay twenty miles southeast of Paris – only to find that in the course of the park's construction, with the fall of the Berlin Wall, the break-up of Yugoslavia, history itself had shifted on its axis.

And of course all the uncertainty and anxiety about the eastern boundary arises precisely because, as Norman Davies again points out, Europe is not, strictly speaking, a continent at all – is not, to use the cognate English term, 'self-contained' – but is merely a peninsula, an outcrop of the world's greatest landmass.

And I am reminded here of another mighty literary figure, Albert Camus, whose work was a godsend to many of us in our Northern Irish nowhere of the late 1970s. Writing during the closing months of the Second World War, which of course like most of the twentieth century's biggest threats to Europe did not come from the east at all, Camus addresses the same question of definition. In the second of his *Letters to a German Friend* he talks about the 'idea of Europe' as opposed to the 'coloured spot [the Nazis have] annexed on temporary maps'. Europe's real frontiers, he goes on with admirable imprecision, are 'the genius of a few and the heart of all its inhabitants'.

I first read Albert Camus at school. I first read Norman Davies in the late summer of 2000, on my return to Belfast from the Literature Express, a project originating in Berlin, which took 106 writers on a seven-week odyssey from Lisbon to Berlin itself, via Spain, France, Belgium, northern Germany, the Baltic states, Russia, Belarus and Poland. And I had chosen Davies's *Europe* out of the many hundreds of books on the subject in part because I knew he was an authority on Poland, the country which, after my month and a half on the Literature Express, I decided I most needed to find out about.

Poland then was still in the middle of protracted negotiations over its application to join the European Union, was still for the moment *east*. On one early detour into Malbork on our way to Kaliningrad from Hanover, the Literature Express had had to sit for an hour on a bridge across the Oder while entry papers were checked. By some extraordinary coincidence a thunderstorm broke at almost the exact moment that the border guards gave us the signal to proceed; the resultant rain mistier than an iron curtain, but atmospherically every bit as effective. Two days later, as we crawled into Kaliningrad after another border shakedown, a Croatian writer observed, 'The time machine is working: we have gone from the seventies to the fifties.'

I laughed along with him, though in truth I already felt myself smitten by the country we were leaving behind. More than smitten: over the months that followed I became evangelical about Poland, talking about it with the zeal of the convert to whoever would listen. Without understanding Polish history there was no understanding European history and of course without understanding European history there was no breaking away finally from the politics of the past, no freedom, you might say, from folklore. I was so fond of Poland I kept pinned to the notice board above my desk the fine I had received in Warsaw for jaywalking in my distracted state. (The fine I had received and had left the country without paying: there is a limit even to my distraction.)

A little under four years later, on 1 May 2004, Poland was finally admitted to the European Union and, the year after that, direct flights began between Belfast and Warsaw; direct and, more to the point, cheap.

And, since I have, however glancingly, just invoked the first half of the title of this lecture, let me in similar fashion now invoke the second: one of the greatest populist measures of recent decades has surely been the deregulation of the airline industry. Set aside for a moment the potentially disastrous environmental impact of all those short-haul flights; set aside for a moment, too, the cram-them-in approach to customer service; nothing has done more to encourage European integration than the budget airlines. Actually, if they were to rebrand the European Union as the *Easyjet* Union and offer mini-weekend-break membership, I am certain that Britain would be transformed overnight into a nation of EU enthusiasts.

I am being facetious, of course, but there is a more serious underlying point.

Europe was always seen as something we in the United Kingdom of Great Britain and Northern Ireland could opt into. Add to this the fact that Northern Ireland, like the rest of the island, has always been a net exporter of people and you will appreciate something of the shock that was experienced when it became clear that the European traffic was two-way, that there were people – quite large numbers of people in fact – who were opting into living in our curious European outpost: Portuguese, Lithuanians, Latvians, and above all, Poles. In less than three years the Polish population of Northern Ireland has gone from round about zero to more than 30,000, or to something close to 2 per cent of the population. More people now have Polish as a first language than have Irish, but then again more people have Cantonese than have Irish.

Even before the recent immigration boom, Belfast was acquiring the unenviable reputation of being the racist capital of Europe. The Northern Irish Peace Process has brought a rapid increase in house prices – more rapid actually than the Peace Process itself. Rents too have been pushed up so that many of the new immigrants have been obliged to look for accommodation in 'hard-to-let' (and therefore cheap) parts of town. In the case of the Poles in particular this has sometimes had the effect of upsetting the religious or sectarian balance: Poland is a predominantly Catholic country; the hardest-to-let areas in Belfast tend to be working-class Protestant areas. There have been innumerable incidents: windows broken, threats made, even houses set on fire. It makes not a blind bit of difference of course to the person on the receiving end of it, but it has not always been immediately clear whether a particular attack is an example of new-style xenophobia, or old-style religious bigotry.

I recently witnessed something of this confusion myself. My wife is from Cork: the People's Republic of Cork as some of its citizens like to refer to it. Earlier this year, my wife's family came to visit us in Belfast: parents, brother, sister, their spouses and children. Not so many years ago this might have been cause for concern: southern Irish cars have very distinctive number plates. People from Cork in particular have very distinctive accents. The part of Belfast we live in has a distinctively *Ulster* British hue: red, white and blue flags on the lampposts, red, white and blue paint on the walls. This being 2007, however, we all walked out to a neighbourhood restaurant on the Saturday evening and walked back, a little more unsteadily, a few hours later. My wife's brother and her sister's husband – the least unsteady of us all – had got quite far ahead of the rest of us when they suddenly found themselves confronted by a group of youths who had overheard them talking.

'Fuck away off back where you came from, you Polish bastards,' the youths said. My brothers-in-law were almost too astonished to be intimidated (the fear, as always, came much, much later). 'Polish?' they said when we had caught up with them and the youths had melted away. 'They thought these were *Polish* accents?'

Well 'thought' is probably too reasoned a word, but there would appear to have been an automatic identification of something that sounded clearly 'other' with the new object of suspicion – recent EU immigrants – rather than with the old 'folkloric' enemy south of the Irish border.

This incident occurred about fifty metres from the headquarters of the avowedly populist Democratic Unionist Party, founded and led by the Reverend Ian Paisley, who was once, infamously, ejected from the European Parliament for interrupting an address by Pope John Paul II with shouts of 'antichrist'. ('No Pole In Strasbourg' either, obviously.)

Ian Paisley was also the founder and long-time leader of the Free Presbyterian Church, whose website not so very long ago carried the headline 'Threat to Protestant Ulster' above a story alleging that priests were helping immigrants get their names on to the Northern Ireland electoral register. Of course, as citizens of the European Union, the immigrants have every right to be on the register, but it is their Catholicism and not, primarily, their nationality that the website is alarmed by. Whether explicitly or implicitly, however, the suggestion is made again that immigration could 'tip the balance' of local politics.

Against this it is important to add that there have been attempts by Protestant community activists (often a euphemism for 'former paramilitaries') to reduce racist attacks. In one instance, in the town of Lisburn, residents have been reminded that Polish pilots played a vital role during the Battle of Britain, though quite what the implications of this are for any Germans hoping to immigrate to Northern Ireland is anyone's guess. In words not often associated with Northern Ireland in recent years, the scheme has been praised as a model of toleration and integration.

And there have been other encouraging signs of late. The last decade in Northern Ireland has seen a transformation of the police, from the Royal Ulster Constabulary – 'the RUC dog of repression', in another famous song from that first Stiff Little Fingers album – to the Police Service of Northern Ireland (PSNI). The PSNI has what is referred to as a 50-50 recruitment policy, that is equal numbers of Catholics and Protestants, to redress historic under-representation of the former. Figures released at the beginning of 2007 reveal that almost 1,000 Poles currently living in Northern Ireland applied to join. There was even a special recruitment drive in Poland itself, prompting some to joke that in time the name will officially change again to the *Polish* Service of Northern Ireland. (Stranger things have happened: look at the dominance of the Irish in the New York police of the last century.)[1]

Now I am conscious that in allowing my mind to wander down paths of its own choosing, I have ended up sticking very close to home. Perhaps this is only to be expected. You know the old dictum: all politics is local politics.

I hope, though, there is more to it than that. I have been trying to use the place that I know best to illustrate a general point, a point that Albert Camus makes much, much more eloquently (again, sadly, only to be expected) in that second wartime *Letters to a German Friend* when he writes, 'Europe will

---

1. I spoke too soon. Figures released in the *middle* of 2007 revealed that only two Polish citizens passed the first stage of the PSNI entrance exam. Neither turned up for stage two.

need to be re-established. *It will always need to be re-established.* (My emphasis.)

This is indubitably not, to Camus, a question of deciding where to draw the borderlines, between what is east, say, and what is west: what is 'us' and what is 'other'. It is rather something more akin to an internal renewal, a perpetual revision or reimagining, which, in a curious way, brings me back again to where I began: speculating on failures of imagination or punctuation.

Punctuation in English can also refer to one of the periods of rapid change that interrupt periods of stasis in the evolutionary theory of 'punctuated equilibrium'. I think it is safe to say that Europe – the European Union in particular – has experienced just such a 'punctuation' in recent times. And there is more to come, with all the risks and all the opportunities that will bring.

In the final page of *Europe*, written in 1992, Norman Davies echoes Camus: 'The European Union in the West and the successor states in the East,' he writes, 'must redefine their identities, their bounds, and their allegiances. Somehow, at least for a time, a new equilibrium may be found … Europe is not going to be fully united in the near future, but it has a chance to be less divided than for generations past. If fortune smiles, the physical and psychological barriers will be less brutal than at any time in living memory.'

In 2007, elections were held in Northern Ireland. As expected, the parties that emerged strongest were, in second place, Sinn Féin, led by Gerry Adams, and, in first place (despite the scaremongering of the Free Presbyterian website), the Reverend Ian Paisley's Democratic Unionists. On the surface the election result indicated that the religious, some would say tribal, blocs in Northern Ireland were as far apart as ever, further apart perhaps than they had been when the whole sorry saga of what we call the Troubles began. There were, however, some interesting pointers to a less divided future. The non-sectarian Alliance Party saw its vote rise for the first time in a decade. One of the party's candidates, Anna Lo, became the first member of the country's Chinese community to be elected to the Northern Ireland Assembly. Anna Lo herself believes that many in the Chinese community had never voted at all before.

The weekend after the election, Stiff Little Fingers played in the Ulster Hall in the centre of Belfast, a month short of thirty years after they first formed. They played their debut album in its entirety. I wasn't there. (I had a deadline to meet: this lecture to deliver to my German translator.) But I'd like to think some of our new Polish neighbours were in amongst the ageing punks, singing along to 'Here We Are Nowhere'. We're still two-thirds of the way to the North Pole, but thanks in no small measure to the people from other parts of Europe – other parts of the *world* – who have chosen to make their home here, we're somewhere a little bit different from where we used to be.

Published in the *European Studies Journal*, Vol.28, 2010

Is this Central?

I want to start with a confession: I have often fantasized about amassing large amounts of money in return for very small amounts of work. At the height of the 'dot-com bubble' I dreamed up a company called 'off-centre dot com', which I imagined would become the first online stop for the many, many millions of would-be travellers who did not live a short taxi ride from Heathrow or Charles de Gaulle. In a more refined version of this fantasy, there would have been on the site a little sidebar – a light-hearted-aside bar – calculating all journeys from Belfast's Central Station, or as I hoped it might be persuaded to rename itself in light of potential commercial benefits and in light, frankly, of geographical veracity, Off-central Station.

For any of you unfamiliar with our city, Central is that large, pink-clad shed of a building perched beside a bridge over the River Lagan, with large groups of perplexed-looking people outside it wondering where the promised centre has disappeared to while opportunistic taxi drivers attempt to steer them towards illegally parked black cabs.

Unfortunately for my entrepreneurial ambitions, and my bank balance, I spent so long entertaining myself with sidebars, with trying to work out the keystroke for an off-centre dot, that the historical moment passed and the dot-com bubble burst.

The moral of this? Never go into business with a writer.

And after the confession, a caveat: I wanted to say that I am a product of the periphery, a child of the suburbs, but every time I want to say I am *anything* I think of a sentence from a letter written by Rosa Luxemburg to her friend Henriette Holst: 'Don't believe me in general. I'm different at every moment, and life is made up only of moments.' (That, by the way, is Rosa Luxemburg born in the town of Zamosc, 247km southeast of Warsaw, which you might think is about as peripheral as you can get.) What we think of as our past is the line we try to draw connecting these discrete moments. Be that as it may, I, or a person that once was I, grew up on what was then the limit of Belfast city. A short distance up the main road from the shops at Finaghy crossroads was a sign welcoming you to the neighbouring borough of Lisburn.

One of my earliest memories is of boarding the train at Finaghy halt, about a hundred yards north of the crossroads, for the journey into the centre of town, to the Great Northern Railway station – the GNR – at Great Victoria Street (*everything* was great back then). Now that really was a station. Not perhaps on a par, say, with the station in Antwerp – so memorably described by the narrator of W. G. Sebald's final novel, *Austerlitz*, to step into whose entrance hall is to be 'seized by a sense of being beyond the profane, in a cathedral consecrated by international traffic and trade' – but a building nevertheless with an aura of anticipation, a building which, like Antwerp, in Sebald's rendering of it, 'far-exceeded its purely utilitarian function'. You felt when you got off the train at the GNR that you had arrived somewhere, as opposed to Central Station's middle of nowhere.

I worried that I might be overstating the station's remoteness. It is, after all, less than half a mile from the back of the City Hall, but just the other night I met a friend up from Dublin for the Belfast Festival who told me that she had been standing on the footpath outside, scratching her head, only to be told by one helpful passer-by, 'Sure you're not in Belfast at all, you'd have been better getting out at Portadown.' No, the most that you were ever likely to feel in Central Station was that you were somewhere that could withstand a five-hundred-pound car bomb. I don't know if bomb-proofing was part of the architect's brief, but it was part of the station's folklore and was certainly of a piece with what I might call the prevailing Bunker School of Troubles Architecture.

If, as is reasonable to assume, the fabric of our towns and cities not only reflects the builders' preoccupations and expectations, and by builders I mean planners, architects, financiers public and private, but also contributes to the citizen's sense of self, then Central, completed in 1976 (the same year, pleasingly, as David Bowie's *Station to Station* was released), was the perfect expression of my (less than golden) early teenage years: mistrustful to the point of paranoid. Actually, talking of golden years, the playwright Owen McCafferty, an exact contemporary of mine, said to me recently that we lived in a very black and white world when we were teenagers, then after a moment added, 'and we should have been living in colour.'

Just four years before Central bowed-in, another building, standing at approximately the same distance from the city centre was completed, or the extension to an existing building: the Ulster Museum. That is, approximately the same distance in another direction. In an article by Mark Hackett for the *Architectural Research Quarterly*, this 'transformative concrete extension' is described by Paul Clarke as 'an icon to a period when architecture addressed at the very centre of its responsibility, the *optimism* of modern life, culture and public space'.

What a change four years can bring; well, four years and several hundred car bomb attacks.

That Ulster Museum extension, coincidentally, was inspired by (and I again have to thank Mark Hackett for this) the memorial to Rosa Luxemburg in Berlin, designed by Mies van der Rohe and destroyed by the Nazis, whose Freikorps forebears had of course murdered Rosa Luxembourg in the first place.

Belfast has done its best to embrace Central Station in the intervening three and a half decades, albeit with call centres and car parks and the rear ends of hotels; and, by dint of successive renovations and refurbishments, that Central Station has done its best to, well, 'embrace' travellers might be stretching it. Rather, Central Station offers you the equivalent of the hug two men meeting perform who aren't entirely sure that hugging is what two men meeting are supposed to do.

Talking of men meeting, I have already mentioned the taxi drivers outside Central Station. New arrivals in the city may have wondered at the peculiarities of our private hire system, may have wondered at it indeed from the back of the taxi to which they were led and then in which they were abandoned while the driver went off to find another four passengers with whom to fill up his vehicle. These newcomers – and those resident here who have nevertheless been gulled by the ploy, and who among us hasn't? – might be interested to know that in the years before 1847, the year that the Victoria Channel was opened, improving access to the town from Belfast Lough (and creating incidentally the Queen's Island aka in 2011-speak the 'Titanic Quarter'), shipping had more often than not to anchor, three miles out along the serpentine Lagan, at the Pool of Garmoyle, there to await a favourable tide. Smaller vessels known as gabbards would take impatient passengers up to town for 6d. And when every seat had been filled, the gabbard pilots would call out for standing passengers at thruppence.

The taxi men at the doors of Central Station are those pilots' direct descendants. You might feel when you pay your fare, when you all *individually* pay your fare, as though you have been taken for a different kind of ride than you were hoping for, but that is a living-history premium you are paying.

Some people spot trains. I, you might have guessed by now, spot stations. One of my favourites is Flinders Street in Melbourne. I like the story that the plans for it got mixed up on a desk in its London architect's office with the plans for Victoria Station in Bombay or Mumbai, today's Chhatrapati Shivaji Terminus. Seeing Flinders Street on my first – my only – visit to Australia, however, my thought was that it had been modelled on one of the great Mittel-European train stations, say Prague, a city I had at that time only visited in the novels of Franz Kafka and Milan Kundera. Indeed, Kundera's *The Unbearable Lightness of Being* opens with the arrival at Prague Railway Station of Tereza, one of the novel's central characters, from her home in a small town 200km from the capital.

Ever open to distraction, I got up from my desk while thinking about this and went back to that novel hoping for an evocation of the station, but found none. I did, however, find the following passage that seemed to me to be germane: 'Toilets in modern water closets,' writes Kundera at the end, it has to be said, of a pretty unpleasant sex scene involving Tereza and a man, an engineer, she has only minutes before met, toilets 'rise up from the floor like white water lilies. The architect does all he can to make the body forget how paltry it is … The bathroom in the old working-class flat' – where this pretty unpleasant sex scene took place – 'on the outskirts of Prague was less hypocritical: the floor was covered with gray tile and the toilet rising up from it was broad squat and pitiful. It did not look like a water lily; it looked like what it was: the enlarged end of a sewer pipe'.

Belfast Central Station, to return to something resembling a point, despite those various clumsy attempted embraces, is no water lily. It remains a point of entry and exit. It does its job. If it is romance you are after, you had better bring your own.

I recently co-wrote the script for a film that has just finished shooting, *Good Vibrations*. It is set in Belfast of the late 1970s when Central was still a recent addition to the skyline and when a new breed of romantics began to make an appearance in our city: punks (and the more time passes the more punk looks like a romantic movement or moment, with and without the capital R). Access to Belfast city centre was at that time controlled by security gates, the majority of which were shut by 9 p.m. and several of which, incidentally, mapped on to the gates in the rampart around the seventeenth-century town. And there were other forms of control. Although we now have our own not-much-loved version of the Boulevard Périphérique, Belfast's road system historically resembled a bicycle wheel, with a series of roads converging on the centre. It was possible by abandoning four or five cars at strategic points to bring the entire city's traffic to a standstill. Not just possible, but regularly done, usually on a Friday.

One of the favourite spots for abandoning vehicles was the railway bridge at Finaghy. On another occasion a bomb exploded prematurely on a train just short of Finaghy Halt, killing a primary school friend of mine.

There were at that time – as I was once told by the owner of a bar now buried beneath the Victoria Square shopping centre

– no more than five or six people living within the city-centre security zone and three of them were above the bar where we were speaking: my informant, his mother and his father. The young people who started in the closing years of the 1970s to venture along those spokes into town at night found a place whose heart had been bombed – and squeezed – out of it. The bars that they congregated in, on the port side of the security gates, were among the dingiest the city had to offer. 'There's nothing for us in Belfast,' Stiff Little Fingers famously sang in 'Alternative Ulster'.

This is not how it is supposed to be. A more common late seventies' teen experience would be that related by former Teardrop Explodes singer and self-proclaimed druid Julian Cope in his memoir *Head-On*, an everyday story of a boy growing up nowhere in particular, in this case Tamworth in Staffordshire, being seduced by music into wishing he lived somewhere more particular, in this case Liverpool, and the difficulties he encounters along the way, for instance in his choice of further education college:

CF Mott College wasn't in Liverpool, not even in fucking Liverpool. Sure it looked like Liverpool on my father's AA Road Map of the British Isles, but on closer inspection it was in a place called Prescot, about twelve miles out of the city centre. That was like being in Watford and calling it London. Or being in Walsall and calling it Birmingham. Or being in East Berlin and calling it fucking West Berlin. Why was I never at the centre of things ... ? I always seemed to be watching ... nobody would actually invite me in.

And here in a similar vein Siouxsie Sioux, leading light of the so-called Bromley contingent, early adopters of the Sex Pistols, who made the acquaintance of her future bandmates, the Banshees, on the train up to London and whose imagination was fired as much by architecture – Art Nouveau and Art Deco, the Rainbow Room at Biba – as music: 'I always gravitated towards the city, I hated suburbia. Some people stuck to their local town, like Bromley. You could hang out there and feel pretty grown-up. But I hated it. I thought it was small and narrow-minded.'

It is couched rather differently but, at risk of sounding bathetic, it is possible to hear the same frustration in the words of Stephen Dedalus, in Joyce's *A Portrait of the Artist as a Young Man*: 'When the soul of a man is born in this country there are nets flung at it to hold it back from flight', possible to hear the same longing to be at the centre of things in the 'Welcome, O life!' with which at the novel's end he salutes his imminent departure for Paris.

From which, of course, he has returned disillusioned by the time *Ulysses* opens, a mere fifteen months later, when he is to be found living in a Martello tower in Sandycove, which Buck Mulligan, the principal tenant, refers to as the *omphalos*, the centre of the world.

You know the story of the *omphalos*: Zeus orders two swift-flying eagles be released from the most easterly and westerly parts of the known world – of the world known to the Greeks who dreamt him up. Where the eagles meet is the centre.

Where matters of centre and periphery are concerned, in other words, it all depends on where you're starting from.

Stephen views Buck Mulligan with disdain, but nevertheless in appropriating the narrative architecture of the *Odyssey*, Joyce places Dublin at the heart of both human and literary endeavour. The novel with Dublin built into it has, over the course of a century, been incorporated into the city it portrays, a city that, as of 2010, carries the designation 'UNESCO City of Literature', one of only four cities so designated in the world, although more recent events have served to put both the Irish and the Greek *omphaloi* in their places on the periphery – the *southern* periphery, as it has been referred to repeatedly throughout this week's economic summit meetings in Brussels — at the mercy of the European Central Bank.

In the early 1980s the Disney Corporation decided to site its first European theme park in the very centre of Europe, and with the late twentieth-century equivalent of swift-flying eagles, worked out that that centre lay 30km southeast of Paris in Marne la Vallee, a contention that only held for as long as Europe remained divided into eastern and western blocs. Forget Zamosc — even Warsaw, according to the Disney calculation, was on the extreme edge.

Zamosc is sometimes referred to as the Pearl of the Renaissance, the Padua of the East (shades there perhaps of Belfast's former ever-so-slightly aggrandising appellation, 'Athens of the North'). Its great market square — 100 metres by one 100 metres — is flanked by sixteenth-century Armenian tenement houses and, since 1992, the town has enjoyed UNESCO world heritage status. If you live in the village of Bozy Dar, Zamosc is the big smoke. It all depends on where you are starting from.

One of the joys of train journeys is the gradual onset of the urban, a feeling of concentration, of mounting possibility (what are all those streets, after all, if not invitations?), or indeed, in the other direction, a shaking off of the city. Travel by train from Gare de Lyon to Disneyland Paris and at a certain point, somewhere about Bussy Saint-Georges, the trackside furniture begins to acquire mouse ears, so that it is hard to know where Paris ends and Disney begins, or, to invoke Rosa Luxemburg again, hard to know, from one moment to the next, which to believe in.

Disneylands of course have the infrastructure as well as the gravitational pull of traditional cities. In the wake of the September 11th attacks on New York and Washington, special anti-terrorism barriers were installed at Disneyworld in Florida, capable apparently of withstanding a twenty-thousand-pound bomb, which you would have to say beats the architectural defences of Central into a cocked hat. Even 'absolutely fake cities', to use Umberto Eco's term, can, it seems, have authentic fears of acts of terror. That is after all the point of terrorism: there is no inside and no outside, the battlefront is wherever the terrorist happens to fetch up next: a Bali nightclub, a Baghdad marketplace, Chhatrapati Shivaji Terminus.

Terrorism has a way of equalising all places. In the aftermath of an explosion, everywhere resembles everywhere else: the hands tearing at the rubble, the ambulances trying to force their way through shocked and dazed bystanders, the burning cars, the curtains flapping in the glassless windows, the papers blowing around.

For an intense moment, as the breaking news banners roll, the seat of the explosion itself is a kind of *omphalos*: 'Now you are all looking at us.'

Of course the world will only look with interest for so long: attention, like buildings, can be bomb-proofed: ratings as much as an outbreak of reason probably saved Belfast from a worse battering in the 1980s. It drifted to the periphery of even its home-grown bombers' minds. Give them a Canary Wharf spectacular any day.

To say that Belfast is changing is nothing new. It has been changing for the better for thirty years. I miss the bar that used to house three of the five people living in the city centre, but only a zealot would begrudge the fact that there are dozens of flats a minute or two's walk from where that bar used to be, or miss the gates and fences that kept our centre so underpopulated for so long. With those gates gone, the centre has shifted back towards the port – the late twentieth-century periphery – the once thriving, several times dead, now thriving streets and entries off High Street and Waring Street. It has shifted indeed to the very streets frequented by those late seventies' romantics, the punks: romantics and, as it turns out, architectural conservationists: witness, or better still visit, the wonderful Oh Yeah Centre, situated in a warehouse on Gordon Street, where you will find among the rehearsal rooms and recording facilities a museum containing artefacts such as the studded leather jacket worn by Greg Cowan of seminal Belfast punk band the Outcasts.

It may shift still further: the Titanic Quarter may well – in fact almost certainly will – prove to be substantially more than the disaster theme park suggested by its name and museum 'signature building'. Not too many decades from now people may laugh at my referring to the station on East Bridge Street as Off-Central. I'm not proud: I will accept laughs retrospectively, even posthumously.

The centre finally is not spatial but temporal. We whose opinion is sought today will eventually, and it will feel to us like the day after tomorrow, experience the banishment of age. There is no way back from that periphery. (The writer Carlo Gébler has a very simple three-word formula for how best to exact revenge on critics: 'outlive the fuckers'.)

And those citizens of Belfast who come after me may well judge Central Station differently. No water lily certainly, but no sewer pipe either.

My children love it. It is, along with the equally unprepossessing George Best City Airport, their place of farewells and welcome-homes. Actually, just after my youngest daughter was born I was at the ticket desk when a friend who worked in Central, Ken Pringle – whose voice it is that tells you when you are approaching Newry and requests that you refrain from putting feet on seats – saw me and asked what we had had, boy or girl. A girl, I said: Miranda. 'Like *The Tempest*,' he said.

'Like *The Tempest*,' I agreed. And as I walked away towards the gate for the Dublin train his voice came over the tannoy.

'Oh, brave new world, Miranda.'

That hath, he didn't say, such stations in it.

Like I say, with Central, it helps if you supply your own romance.

A version of this Lecture to the Architectural Humanities Research Association 'Peripheries' conference was published in the *Dublin Review*, Number 47, Summer 2012.

Olympic Torch

On first glance the torch's Belfast route appears to be a homage to my brother Paul. For years, whenever friends or friends of friends or members of the Patterson Diaspora came to town for the first time, or just the first time in a long time, Paul was on hand in fair weather and foul to give them The Tour (a tour they were nearly too shy to come right out and ask for): north Belfast, Shankill Road, Springfield Road, the near east ... His only competition then was from the black cabs whose drivers doubled as guides, with perhaps a leaning to this side or to that depending on where in town you picked them up. Now you cannot move in Belfast for tour buses or tour-bus ticket sellers. Many of the buses carry the Titanic livery, because since the turn of the year you cannot move either in Belfast for things Titanic. (The Olympic flame, needless to say, takes in Titanic Belfast® too. And, no, you didn't misread that: they've finally done it, they've trademarked our town.) This proliferation of tours, and tourists, is not wholly or even mostly a bad thing, though I should perhaps confess at this point that I recently led my own tour around 1830s' Belfast (motto: 'If it wasn't there then you're not going there now'). For far too long the only people who came here – friends of friends and Diaspora aside – were journalists and conflict junkies. Now we send our politicians and former combatants to other conflict zones to teach people there how to emulate our journey to peace.

It is a journey that the Olympic relay is clearly designed to reflect. The route, like my brother Paul's tour, takes in some of Belfast's most notorious 'interfaces' – Duncairn Gardens, for example, and Lanark Way, a favourite escape route in days gone by for loyalist gunmen. In both these areas improvements have begun to be made; barriers have been softened, if not yet removed.

More problematically, the route also skirts the site of the former Girdwood army barracks, off the Antrim Road, twenty-seven acres of inner-city real estate whose redevelopment has been the subject of protracted negotiations between the two main parties in our mandatory coalition, Sinn Féin and the DUP. A fortnight ago the plans were unveiled at a photocall on the Girdwood site, to which, perversely, media access was restricted. The single photograph that was released shows quite clearly two separate areas of housing, one at the Protestant lower Oldpark end and the other, a quarter of a mile distant, at the Catholic New Lodge. To many here it looks like an old-style sectarian carve-up – 'gerrymandering' we used to call it – only now with two parties colluding.

Actually, to be truly symbolic of Belfast 2012, the Olympic relay ought to include a three-legged pairing of Sinn Féin and DUP ministers, by turns bickering and whispering in one another's ears.

And if by chance the going got too tough for them, they could always hop on a bus, or give my brother Paul a call.

Guardian Online, 3 June 2012

Peace Procession

On Tuesday night I took part in a debate, organised by the Royal Irish Academy, in Belfast's City Hall, on whether we in Northern Ireland should continue to commemorate the past. That lunchtime I had stood at City Hall's front gates at a rally to the memory of David Black, a citizen of ours murdered last week by the latest version of the IRA.

The two things combined have led me to one conclusion. It is time to declare an end to the Peace Process.

I do not mean by this that it is time to give in to the 'men of violence' (imagine us doing that, here, in Northern Ireland ...), still less do I mean I want to see a return to the 'dark days'.

I mean simply that the term itself has got to go.

I say the events of yesterday led me to this conclusion, but it would be more accurate to say they led me back. It has occurred to me before, as it must surely have occurred to a great many people here, that the Process is part of what continues to ail us.

The Process says we are not there yet, but it leaves the decision of where *there* is to the professional Processors. It is not in my gift. It is not in yours. We are left to hope that where the Processors eventually tell us we should be and where we would like to be coincide.

Worse, looking in the other direction, the Process has a way of folding into itself historical events that seem to fly in the face of its own purported logic. That is how we came by such oxymoronic phrases as 'fighting for peace'. Who knew that that's what all those killings in the last third of the twentieth century were for?

Previously, though, I had wondered how we could be persuaded to relinquish something that in its early years did serve us well, and continues to serve the Processors, not least on the international stage.

And then yesterday I thought there would need to be an event to bring the curtain down. A big event – an enormous event: a Peace Procession, no less.

Not a march for peace, but a march in confirmation of peace. Because the dissidents will not be Processed away. There has always been a strand, or strain, of Irish republicanism that is resistant to political good practice and example. The Process indeed plays into the mouths of those who would claim there is unfinished business here.

Like the Copts choosing a Pope, the choice of where to start the Peace Procession would be effected by a blindfolded child, only instead of drawing a name from a barrel he or she would stick a pin in a map: *there*. Everyone who lived in that particular *there* would be invited to join in, to walk or otherwise convey themselves at walking pace as far as they felt able. The Procession would go down every road, in and out of every street. And at any point along the way anyone who wanted to could call a halt and bear witness to what happened in that spot. To what they saw, what they suffered, what they knew, what they did.

And then the Procession would move on (imagine the Olympic Torch relay; multiply it; keep multiplying), down the next road and in and out of the next street, until all the stories that were there to be told were told.

That would be our legacy. A map of words.

It would, I realize, take a long, long time, but not anything like as long as the current Peace Process has taken, and unlike the current Peace Process we could be confident that it would, one day, reach its conclusion.

Instead of Political Process we would have Politics, instead of Peace Process we would have tomorrow and the day after tomorrow and the day after that again.

We would still have our past, go there still in our memories, our hearts – our *arts* – and our City Hall debates, but our elected representatives could no longer have recourse to it to explain our present inadequacies. And no one, but no one, could ever again claim when levelling a gun or leaving a bomb to be finishing business that we had all agreed was unfinished.

Let's start the end here.

The Irish Times, 8 November 2011

The Message

So, it's 1977, bleak Belfast days, and nights. My friends and I, we don't get out much: sneaky drinks in the dark of the playing fields, a walk around the estate hoping to bump into girls. Now and then we chance the chippy, dodgy not because of gunmen or bombers, but because of other – bigger – bored local lads like us. Bigger bored lads like Hambo. Who has hit me once already for fighting with a younger boy whose sister knew Hambo's sister. (The Tudors had less complicated genealogies.) This particular night the scout who has been sent to peer around the corner returns to tell us the chippy is all clear. We get our chips. (Our *chip*, a load of deep-fried potatoes here being singular and us being singularly and collectively broke.) We stand on the low wall facing the chippy – because that is what you do, stand on the wall, not the footpath – reading the graffiti on the grey painted bricks, graffiti which appears to confirm what we have long feared, that while we are sneaking drinks or walking around the estate, everyone else is having sex. Lots of it. There are some helpful diagrams, should we ever get round to it ourselves. And there is one brick that is dense with text in neat black marker. I lean forward to read it: 'Hambo is a dead man, signed the Provos'. Ha! It's so funny I read it aloud. 'I mean,' I say, 'as if the Provos would come round here to write on a brick. As if they would write "signed the Provos".' No one laughs. They can't have heard. I read it again. If it is possible for people who have not laughed to laugh less, they laugh less. They are not even looking at me. They are looking past me, at Hambo, who is swaggering along – *Hambo*-ing – and sticking out his chin. 'Hambo is a *what* signed *who*?' he says. I point at the brick. (I am sure it is only in my memory that my finger droops.) Hambo stops between me and the wall. I don't see the punch coming, but I hear it, between my ears – an actual *biff*. I blink, in surprise as much as anything, but I don't cry, much to Hambo's annoyance. 'You're not crying? Try this …' And there is the *biff* again, louder than before. I cover my face with my hands. I make the crying sound. Through my fingers I see him take out a marker of his own. 'The Provos are dead men,' he writes. 'Signed Hambo.'

Short Cuts, Radio 4, 30 May 2013

Travels with My Brick

Late in 2012 I had an email from the Fermanagh Writers inviting me to conduct a workshop in Enniskillen the following spring or early summer. After much to-ing and fro-ing about dates, we agreed on Saturday 15 June. A couple of weeks later David Cameron announced that the G8 summit would be held in the Lough Erne Resort on the outskirts of Enniskillen on 17–18 June. After more to-ing and fro-ing, the Fermanagh Writers and I decided to go ahead with the workshop as planned. Wasn't it one of the ideas behind the choice of location for the summit, after all, to show that Northern Ireland was open for business?

I spent Friday afternoon preparing – I would do Jeffrey Eugenides on *Middlesex*; I would do an extract from the *Odyssey*, another from *The Third Man* novella. On Saturday morning, about ten minutes before I left the house, it occurred to me I might need something more.

I lifted Ciaran Carson's *Belfast Confetti* down from the shelf.

I was travelling to the workshop by bus – less chance of being held up or diverted, I had thought. I texted the workshop organiser en route: 'Daft question, but is there any chance you could lay your hands on a brick?'

Security was evident, but not obtrusive: a police roadblock about a mile out of Enniskillen; two tooled-up police officers walking through the bus station – pretty tooled-up police officers, it has to be said; a few more Land Rovers than might be expected on a normal Saturday afternoon in June, but no ring of steel, at least not here in the town centre. I was a little disappointed. I had been joking with friends the night before about my going to Enniskillen: imagine all that security for me. What do they think I'm going to do – divulge the secret of fiction? Though in truth the eight people meeting in Enniskillen on Monday and Tuesday could probably teach me a thing or several billion about making things up.

I got to the venue – above the Horse and Saddlers Bar and Restaurant. There were the eight – sorry: *eighteen* – Fermanagh Writers; there was the brick – a local brick, said Ken who had brought it, from Fivemiletown. I set it upright on the table in front of me. I started the workshop. I did Jeffrey Eugenides on *Middlesex*, I did the extracts from the *Odyssey* and *The Third Man*. I still had half an hour to go: I'd been right, I did need something more – I needed the brick.

I asked the writers what they could say about it. The responses were more interesting than I had had in the past. They mentioned materials (cement), texture (roughcast), style (no 'frog' or trough for mortar), size (about six inches I had hazarded, for the first time in my adult life apparently underestimating: it was nine), but they indulged too in a bit of free association. One man told a story about a building site he had once worked on – two tanned young brickies, and a grumpy old fella on the cement mixer. One woman said the brick, in greyness, made her think of a dull dinner-party guest. Actually, she said, it reminded her of one of her previous husbands, which sentence, we all agreed, was a story in itself.

Ken, who had provided the brick, informed us that it was a reject: he had taken a load of them away from the brickworks once when he was building his house. And *The House of Rejected Bricks*, we agreed, was possibly the best title any of us had ever heard.

Finally I opened *Belfast Confetti* and read Ciaran Carson's take on 'Brick', a three and a half page prose diptych, the first part an exploration of the word, its cognates and its peculiarly Belfast usages (half-bricks are an ingredient of the rioter's 'Belfast confetti' from which the book takes its title); the second part an autobiographical vignette of a childhood spent building and destroying miniature cities with his friend Noel.

I lifted the brick from the desk. Any time you think you have nothing to write about, I said, remember this brick. Remember what happens when you bombard it with questions – like splitting the atom – what it yields up. And that was it; the workshop was over. And of course the Fermanagh Writers made a present to me of the brick.

'Let's see how far you get with it,' one woman said as we stepped outside. A police car passed. Not a flicker. 'That's because you are holding it in the same hand as your mineral water,' she said.

Back at the bus station the G4S security man did look askance at me, but said nothing. I had misread the timetable and was an hour early for the bus back to Belfast. I was carrying a nine-inch brick. It was heavy. I decided to stay put. At one stage I parked the brick behind a bench while I went to the toilet. The G4S man looked at me more suspiciously when I walked by without it, more suspiciously still when he passed me sitting on the bench a few minutes later, brick once more on my lap.

As the bus pulled in at last, he approached me. 'You might have trouble getting your travelling companion on,' he said, not at all unpleasantly.

'It's a prop,' I said, 'for a workshop. It's from Fivemiletown.'

He shrugged. 'It's between you and the driver.'

I took out *Belfast Confetti* just in case, folded it open at the relevant page. I had been on the road since nine in the morning, it would be close to eight before this bus reached Belfast. I wanted to be sure I got home.

The driver wanted only to see my return ticket: all in order.

I sat in the last but one seat, the emergency exit, for extra legroom. Extra leg- and brick-room.

Security had grown much more visible in the time that I had been in the Horse and Saddlers. Incoming traffic was backed up close to the Killyhevlin Hotel on the approach to the town. We passed a convoy of Land Rovers,, passed a lay-by where twenty or so PSNI officers stood around waiting to move up. We passed a filling station with half a dozen large black vehicles, windows tinted, in the forecourt, an even larger black vehicle at their centre, even darker windows.

'There's someone, now,' said the man behind me to his (animate) travelling companion. 'That's definitely someone.'

As though he was no one and none of the rest of us anyone either.

('You have a brick,' the same man said to me as he got off in Dungannon. 'From Fivemiletown,' I said, and he gave me a wink.)

My wife had texted to say the police were out in force in Belfast too. We had already agreed she would pick me up from the Europa Bus Centre. There was, besides the G8 and its attendant protests, a big Orange parade in east Belfast where we live: roads were closed, local buses diverted.

I stood inside the doors of the arcade leading to the station, facing the Crown Bar, looking out for the car.

I was holding the brick in the same hand as my phone now. (Shades of Dom Joly, I thought.) I watched a foot patrol, four officers strong, pass south along Great Victoria Street, glancing into bins, into taxis drawn up before the Europa Hotel and the Crown. About ten minutes later (because there *was* traffic disruption: my wife had had to take a big detour), I watched them pass along the street in the opposite direction. A moment after they passed the arcade, a man and woman and their pre-teen daughter came in off the street. The man stared at me, at the brick. I didn't notice him leave again. I had had a text from one of my daughters who was in the car with her mum: 'Nearly there.'

I stepped out onto the pavement and as I did I saw the man talking to the foot patrol, who was turning around, coming back towards me.

The officer with the machine gun strolled over, insofar as anyone with a machine gun slung across her midriff can stroll.

'Is it the brick?' I asked.

'It is the brick,' she said.

I told her it was a prop. I told her it was from Fivemiletown.

One of the other officers had gone round behind me. 'It's a prop,' she called to him. I looked over my shoulder. He didn't look as though he was buying it. I turned back to the officer with the machine gun.

'I've been using Ciaran Carson's "Brick". You set this on the table at the start and ask people what it is then you read "Brick" and suddenly it's more than just a brick ...'

'The power of education,' she said.

'That's right.'

She looked at me, weighing all this up. 'You're not a protestor then?'

'I'm a writer,' I said.

A single nod of the head: clearly the two things in her mind were mutually exclusive, which is one of the more dispiriting aspects of this tale.

Over her shoulder I saw our car. I left her talking to the man and woman and their pre-teen daughter.

I got into the passenger seat.

'What's with the brick?' my own daughter asked.

'Long story,' I said.

Guardian, 22 June 2013

Secretly Canadian

Before I start can I just say a few words: London, London, London, London, London, London, London, London ... Those are for the editors at the BBC who may want to place them strategically throughout this recording, or indeed for anyone who happens to prefer a four-syllable to a two-syllable place name. To quote Chuck Berry in 'My Ding-a-Ling', whose lyrics in retrospect read like a first draft of the Good Friday Agreement, this is a free country, people, you gotta live like you wanna live, ain't nobody gonna bother you if you do.

I thought since this essay was for Radio 3 I ought to include a few music references.

Oh, and I need to add one word more: Legend; because every broadcast from or about Derry in this UK City of Culture year is obliged to say it at least once. Again, I invoke the Chuck Berry clause.

And if those two allusions to the great rock 'n' roller came out as Chuck *London*berry, you'll know that the BBC editors have already been at work. The UK in City of Culture, on the other hand, was me.

For the past almost-decade now the Belfast-based art collective Factotum has published a free monthly newspaper called the *Vacuum*. Each issue is, or was – it occurs to me I haven't seen it for a while – themed. So there was Education, there was Sport, there was Money, Madness – those were separate issues – there was God and Satan – that *was* a double issue, which landed Factotum in hot water with Belfast City Council, its principle funder, due to an article in which one contributor reminisced about wetting herself in church as a child.

This was followed by a Sorry issue that could not have been any less sorry if it had included instructions for folding the paper to form a giant tongue, to be inserted in the reader's cheek.

Another issue – issue 12, if memory serves – was called Down Mexico Way. Now, anyone brought up on twentieth-century popular music knows that Down Mexico Way lies South of the Border. The one follows the other as surely as night follows day. From this, in Belfast parlance, citizens of the Republic of Ireland – *Southerners* – are Mexicans. This was the sense in which the *Vacuum* was using it. And lest this should make any of you uncomfortable, I should tell you that one of the articles, by Colin Graham, is called 'I married a Mexican' and recommends that *everyone* North of the Border marry a Mexican.

For what it's worth, I married a Mexican too, or possibly a Tierra del Fuegian ... she's from Cork.

It is not referred to in the *Vacuum* issue, but some people in Belfast have taken the North American analogy a step further: Derry people by extension are Canadians.

And in case you're still doubting the essentially comic – self-ironic – intent of this, think that if the South is Mexico and Derry is Canada then Belfast, in between, is the land of the free and the home of the brave. You possibly saw some of that freedom and bravery being demonstrated this 12 July with Orange Order supporters dancing on the bonnets of police Land Rovers. I say 'dancing', but if there is one thing that this summer proved definitively to the watching world, it is that Belfast men can't dance.

The song 'South of the Border' incidentally was written – perhaps this should come as no surprise – by an Irish Northerner, Jimmy Kennedy, who until the Beatles came along was the most successful Irish or British songwriter in the United States in the whole of recording history.

Kennedy was born in Cappagh in County Tyrone in 1902 when there was no Border in Ireland, although it had appeared by the time he completed his education in Trinity College Dublin in the early 1920s. Maybe the imposition of this somewhat arbitrary demarcation – Tyrone at one stage was considered for omission from the new Northern Ireland – coloured Kennedy's preoccupations: one of his other big hits was the wartime morale-booster, 'We're Going to Hang Out the Washing on the Siegfried Line'.

The Border, I think, is responsible for my own very partial view of Derry – *distorted* might be a better word – when I was growing up.

To be honest I used to look at Derry on the TV weather map and wonder how it survived way up there so far from Belfast and with a great big black line behind it cutting it off from everywhere else.

I was encouraged in this impression by the adoption in the early 1970s of the postcode system.

People outside of Northern Ireland might not be aware of this, but all Northern Irish postcodes begin BT, for Belfast. BT1 – the *omphalos* – was Belfast city centre. I grew up in BT10 and was already flirting with Lisburn. Derry is BT48. Not as bad as the BT71 that is Jimmy Kennedy's native Cappagh or even the BT94 of certain parts of Enniskillen.

Glenn Patterson

But still, BT48 ... Talk about advertising how far you were
from where the action was?

And yet from a very early age I did find my attention drawn
time and again to Derry and not just on the weather map. Derry
had glamour. Or at least, Derry had Dana. Derry had Bernadette
Devlin, or at least she seemed to belong to Derry.

And – there is no avoiding saying it – Derry invented the riot.
In Belfast we just burned our neighbours out. In Derry riots had
the sweep of a Parisian *événement* ... It is hard to contemplate the
famous slogan on that gable-end at Lecky Street 'You Are Now
Entering Free Derry' without remembering the so-called French
Law of 10 May 1968: 'First disobey, then write on the walls.'

All that changed on Bloody Sunday, of course, but
then everything changed on Bloody Sunday. Colm Tóibín
has written of a turning away from the North by people in
the South in the aftermath, a sense that you either followed
your rage to its logical conclusion – ever greater retaliatory
violence – or you focused your energies elsewhere: Europe
for instance.

That's Europe in the political sense, not Europe, as I thought
of it almost exclusively in those years, in the football sense.

Talking of which ... In the autumn of 1965 Derry City
represented Northern Ireland in the European Cup, having won
the somewhat confusingly named *Irish* League the season before.
After seeing off the Norwegian side, Lyn, in the preliminary
round, City progressed to the first round proper, a round that
mysteriously they never completed.

This was a little before my time watching Irish League
football, but the story as it came down to me was that the Irish
Football Association – the IFA – with its base in Belfast and its
frankly Protestant board – had ruled that the club's Brandywell
stadium was not up to European Cup standard, despite Lyn
having been hosted there a few weeks before.

It was only while thinking about this essay that I looked up the detailed fixture list for the 1965-66 European Cup and discovered that Derry City had lost the away leg of the tie in question to Anderlecht, forty-one-times champions of Belgium, by *nine* goals to nil.

Some people might actually see the decision to ban the second leg as a kindness.

I am tempted to speculate – speculate, that is, with a Belfast-tinted *spec* – that this is an example of the Derry trait of turning defeat into moral victory.

Skip forward five or six seasons, though, and the Brandywell is again being considered unsuitable for hosting matches – or rather unsafe – and Derry City are obliged to play their home games in Coleraine (BT52) or even in Belfast.

I saw them around this time playing Linfield at Windsor Park, BT-single-figures, in what I thought was their final away game there, but come to think could well have been their final home game.

This seems the appropriate moment to mention – and applaud – the IFA's participation in the Derry UK City of Culture programme, not least its Football for Peace and Football Against Racism initiatives and the intriguingly named FA Dealing With the Past Conference, which will no doubt refer to the fact that Derry City left the Irish League finally in October 1972 ... while Chuck Londonberry's (did it happen again?) 'My Ding-a-Ling' was climbing the UK charts, because records in those days did climb the charts, a couple of places at a time over weeks and even months, rather than simply appear in them then just as quickly disappear.

Over the weeks and months that followed Derry City's departure from the Irish League, not just the football team but the city of Derry itself seemed to me, still a child, looking on, to come even further adrift, become more completely other, but by then in any case events in Belfast were outstripping Derry.

To tell you the truth, there were several years when I don't remember giving it a single thought.

And then along came the Undertones.

The Undertones who made absolutely no concessions in how they presented themselves to the world, but walked into TV studios in whatever they would have worn walking into the local youth club, which is exactly the same as what the rest of us were wearing – half-mast jeans, bomber jackets, black brogues or Doc Martens – the Undertones who when asked in an early interview why they didn't follow the then trend for singing in mid-Atlantic accents said that they didn't know anyone who lived in the mid-Atlantic.

In fact if you wanted to read an account of growing up in Derry in those years – growing up anywhere in what some people call the War and other people the Troubles and what I would propose as a compromise we call the Euphemism – you could do far worse than Michael Bradley's *My Life as an Undertone*, originally broadcast on Radio Foyle, where instead of a litany of bombs and bullet-dodging, you will read of skites across to Letterkenny to buy instruments on HP and camping trips over the border in Ballyshannon and Bundoran.

Actually, Michael Bradley's memoir helped open my eyes to something that that black line on the weather map had obscured all these years: Derry is one vast holding camp for Donegal holiday resorts out of season.

The Undertones, I need hardly remind anyone here, released 'Teenage Kicks' in September 1978, and I'll not even be cheap and say that they had to come to Belfast to record it, unless of course it's cheaper of me to say it while claiming I'm not going to say it. Like thousands of other young people across Northern Ireland – hundreds of thousands possibly worldwide – I was galvanised – shaken awake almost – by 'Teenage Kicks'. It wasn't that I hadn't heard music of that sort before, it was just that I hadn't heard anything that good from anyone here, ever.

The song that sealed the deal for me, though, was the follow-up to 'Teenage Kicks', 'Get Over You'. For five years after that the Undertones were the only band for me. I thought that if they were not going to be quite as big as the Beatles they would at least be bigger than Jimmy Kennedy was in his pomp in the USA.

A few years ago the *Guardian* ran a poll of readers' all-time top-five albums. Mine included *Positive Touch*, the Undertones' third album with the exhilarating 'His Good Looking Girlfriend' and the utterly sublime 'Julie Ocean'.

I knew the world was inured to beauty when the single version of 'Julie Ocean' didn't get higher than number forty one in the charts.

I still remember standing by the window of the bookshop where I was working at the time, making a show of rearranging books while straining to hear the chart rundown from the speaker hanging in the doorway of the clothes shop next to us – the outrage I felt, as though it was my own record, when I realized that it hadn't leapt up the charts – leaps as I say were rare, though not entirely unheard of – but had fallen back: off the Radio 1 playlist in effect.

It was probably about then that I started giving serious thought to writing a screenplay, scored by Undertones music. I who at the stage had written a single short story for a school competition entitled 'A World Without Oil: How Can We Cope' and a handful of what I called poems and a poet to whom I was encouraged by a teacher to show them called prose with line-breaks.

Jump Boys, I was going to name it, my Undertones movie, in homage to the boys who always got their grinning chops in front of the cameras when international correspondents were trying to deliver their doleful reports from the streets of war-torn Northern Ireland.

Whether the world will thank them for it – whether indeed any of you will – the Undertones helped set me on the path that led me to the Playhouse tonight.

Who I wish was standing up here with me, however, is a friend of mine ... I say friend of mine ... I mean the wife of the brother of a friend of mine. (When you spend as long as I do sitting in a room by yourself writing you tend to cast the net wide in your definition of friendship.)

This friend-at-a-slight-remove lives in Paris, but she grew up in Ethiopia, at a time in the 1970s that, frankly, in terms of horror, exceeded in almost every measure what was happening here.

But there, as here, people were still going about the necessary, gloriously messy business of being teenagers, and there as here, the radio played a big part.

In 1979 there was one song in particular that caught the imagination: the follow-up to the follow-up to 'Teenage Kicks', 'Jimmy Jimmy'.

So popular was the song there, in fact, that, I seem to recall her saying, it spawned something of a youth movement, kids who were known as Jimmy-Jimmys.

And here's the thing, they had no idea where this record – as redolent of the time and place of its gestation as any of those early Seamus Heaney poems – was coming to them from.

I like to think, though, that her Belfast-born husband was able to enlighten her.

The Undertones? Didn't you know? They're Canadians.

Recorded in the Playhouse, 27 September 2013
Broadcast Radio 3, October 2013

Not Being There[1]
(Or Nil–Two Desperandum)

There is a school of thought in football (and if the words 'school', 'thought' and 'football' made you smirk I'll see you again at the start of the next piece), that says the only real fan is the fan who goes week after week to watch his team in the flesh: the wet Wednesday night Carling Cup away match as well as the home European glamour-ties. By this definition I cannot claim to be a real fan. I have supported Manchester United since I was five years old, yet at the age of forty-five have seen them play only six times, one of them a pre-season friendly in which so many youth team players were fielded I could have been watching a mass *Jim'll Fix-It*[2] for eleven wee lads from down our park.

For maybe twenty of those forty years the only football matches guaranteed to be carried live on television were the FA Cup Final and the annual England v Scotland home international.

1. With a nod to Jerzy Kosinski, who takes it on his thigh, swivels ... In your dreams, Kosinski, in your dreams.
2. We had no idea then; I had no idea still when I wrote this.

113

Of course there were the weekly highlights programmes – *Match of the Day* on BBC, and ITV's *Big Match* – but in those days before Sky removed the limits (and simultaneously narrowed the focus on to the 'big four' clubs), it was rare for any team to feature more than one week in every five or six. Ulster Television took its *Big Match* from London Weekend Television, so Belfast fans could only hope to see United when they came to The Capital and even then it was just as likely you would switch on to find Gillingham entertaining Shrewsbury at the Priestfield Stadium in the old fourth division.[3]

But, then, my father supported Hibernians and Arsenal as a boy and never saw either of them, could hardly imagine the circumstances in which he would get to see them. A match was a composite experience, assembled over two, even three days, starting with the reports in the *Ireland's Saturday Night* aka the *Ulster*. At least when I was growing up we had Radio 2 clearing its Saturday afternoon schedules to bring updates from around The Country, which we listened to while attending matches in our own not-quite-country or even turning out in games ourselves. (Our goalkeeper's second most important task was making sure the transistor behind his goalpost didn't get hit by the ball.) And then there was the legendary Teleprinter, stuttering across the *Grandstand* screen every Saturday from twenty-to-five, leaving a week's worth of hopes dashed or intact in its wake:

4.44 Man United I Southampton stutter-stutter-stutter ohplease-ohplease-ohplease (because the Teleprinter was the first machine I thought was responsive to prayer, or at least to side-deals with God) oh-please-let-it-be-nil-and-I-will-never-again-use-bad-language stutter-stutter-stutter 0.

Thank fuck, Frank Bough!

(Next week, God, next week. Cross my heart and hope to die.)

It was a rare event to arrive at half-past ten on a Saturday night and *Match of the Day* without some knowledge of the

---

3. *More* likely, if anything: the *Big Match's* main commentator, Brian Moore, was a Gillingham director.

afternoon's goings-on. We earned pocket money delivering *Ulsters* (because some institutions are sacrosanct) and even if you tried not to turn to the back page where the English scores were to be found there was always the possibility that a fan of a rival team would give you a broad intimation of how things had gone: 'Jammy bastards the day!' or, more succinctly, 'Up your hole!'

Midweek matches were a different matter. Midweek matches were the source of the newsreader's injunction to 'look away now' if you wanted to avoid seeing the score before the highlights came on. Often, though, it was possible to predict the arc, if not the precise outcome, of a game from just a brief look at the highlights themselves. So Manchester United take on Wolverhampton Wanderers at Molyneux in the replayed quarter final of the FA Cup, March 1976. The highlights start at twenty-five-to-eleven. Wolves are two-up at halftime, but only eight minutes of the forty-minute highlights programme have elapsed. Logic dictates that United will score twice in the second half to force extra time. Logic is sound: United get the two goals and a third in extra time itself to progress to the semi-final. Another important lesson: two-down is not the worst score at halftime, although the reverse is also true: two-up is not the best, two-up is frankly courting disaster. (See, a mere six months after the victory at Wolves, United squandering a two-goal lead at home to Spurs, John Pratt scoring a goal-of-the-season winner.)[4]

---

4. The most famous three-two in United's history was the 1999 UEFA Champions League semi-final second leg away to Juventus. Level at one-one from the first leg (a very late Ryan Giggs goal) United were two down in eleven minutes in Turin. I was watching with my wife in a bar in Montreal where I was reading at the Blue Metropolis Book Festival. (In fact the first thing I had done on arriving in Montreal was identify this as a bar that would be showing the match.) I had never felt more relaxed than I did when that second goal went in, although I did have the double insurance that day of having dreamt the result several months previously. Ask my brother. I told him at a funeral the morning after the dream. And, yes, sadder even than writing about it is dreaming about it. Keane, Yorke and Cole, by the way, the last seven minutes from time. Dream doesn't come close.

Hope, not the other team, is the real opponent. Of course this is true if you are in the ground or not. If you are in the ground, though, you can roar on your support – become the twelfth man (a very, very big twelfth man) – or give vent to your frustration and disapproval, shame the players into greater effort. For the fan following the game at home, often after the event, there is nothing to be done, except perhaps to absent yourself more. Once you have exhausted all your next-week-Gods the only power you have is the power in your legs. You have to know when to walk away, even if it is only to the bathroom. Actually, especially if it is to the bathroom.

Tuesday, 24 April 2007. It is two-two in this season's Champions League semi-final first leg at Old Trafford, United and Milan. This is the hardest kind of two-two to call: United one-up too early – or at least not three-up soon enough afterwards as they were in the previous round at home to Roma – pegged back and then overtaken before halftime. I have been on my feet in the living room since the equaliser in the fifty-ninth minute. The match is now in the ninety-third. There are seconds remaining. Milan break forward and I make a sudden diagonal run out of the living room and into the downstairs toilet. I could not bear to see them score at this late stage. I am having flashbacks to the 1979 FA Cup Final, the so-called 'Five Minute Final': United losing two-nil then two-one, then in the closing minutes drawing level through Belfast's own Sammy McIlroy. In my delirium I ran out of the house meeting my United-supporting neighbour halfway. We hugged, danced around. By the time we got back to our houses it was three-two to Arsenal. Alan-fucking-Sunderland.

The best that can happen, I tell myself tonight over the sound of the water churning in the bowl, is that we will end up with the draw that would have seemed a disaster ninety-three minutes and all this beer ago.

I return to the living room in time to see the replay of the ball beating Dida in the Milan goal for Manchester United's winner in front of the Stretford End. The Milan attack foundered almost as soon as I left the room on Ryan Giggs's tackle (oh, behave), Giggs fed Rooney, who shot first time: three-two with practically the last kick of the game.

Or at least that's how the commentator explains it. A part of me is disappointed to have missed the goal. The larger part, however, knows for a fact that I did not in the truest sense miss the goal at all. If I had stood my ground Giggs would never have made the tackle and the result would have gone the other way: Kaka not Rooney would be lying spread-eagled in celebration on the Old Trafford Turf.

This is not the first time I have conjured a goal from my own bladder.

Wednesday, 7 September 2005, Northern Ireland v England at Windsor Park. I used to be a regular at international home games, through the dark, dark days of the mid and late 1970s — which were actually light, light days, since even weekday matches had to kick off in the afternoon due to Windsor Park's substandard floodlighting — through the early eighties World Cup campaigns, and on into the scoreless run that saw us dubbed Northern Ireland Nil. It isn't the results that have kept me away of late, or even the performances, rather the birth of my children and the complications of Wednesday (or any other) evening at 8 p.m.

Now, when I am desperate for a ticket, it is impossible to get hold of one, the Windsor Park capacity having been reduced by about 95 per cent from the wedged-in days when it was possible to go a full ninety minutes on the terracing without your feet once touching the ground. A lecturer friend is over from Japan. He is keen to watch the match. I suggest he come to my house, although I would far rather watch on my own. That is, I would far rather be somewhere else in the house on my own while the TV is on in the living room. After all I can hardly welcome my friend, set him down with a beer and then run out as soon as England attack, especially given how often England are guaranteed to attack.

For most of the first half they do pretty much nothing else. The only respite is to switch occasionally to the Republic of Ireland v France match on RTÉ, telling myself we are bound to be behind when I turn back. We aren't. This is, for the homebound fan, not good, because worse than England thrashing us would be England sneaking a win just when insanely and despite all your vigilance and experience you had begun once again to hope. I hold off until the seventy-third minute, two minutes after the sort of near miss by Northern Ireland that usually precedes the other side scoring. ('I wonder how significant that could be for Lawrie Sanchez's men at the end of the evening?')

'I must just go to the toilet,' I say.

I stay away for as long as seems decent while leaving open the option of another jog down the hallway in injury time if it's still nil-nil. When I return to the living room my friend is not there. Or at least I notice his absence from the sofa a fraction of a second before I register his presence on the floor in front of the TV. He is, to be precise, on his knees on the floor in front of the TV: on his knees and with his arms around the TV. There is something in there that he does not want to get out. It is a moment or two more before I realize that the something is a goal for Northern Ireland, another five minutes before I can persuade him the goal is safe, we can sit down again.

'We will probably still lose,' I say, 'but at least we scored.'

I am in the kitchen getting more crisps – slowly opening the bag there, slowly – when the final whistle blows.

My friend from Japan is a Glentoran supporter. He chose them several years back because they seemed to be the Northern Irish team best equipped to progress in Europe (or at least not be effectively out after the first round first leg), because of their non-sectarian policy and because they had the best website. Needless to say he had never seen them play.

'We should go to the Oval when you are next over,' I had said to him last time we met. Unfortunately Glentoran were not at home while he was in town on this occasion, but three days after the Northern Ireland game we travelled from east to north Belfast to see his team take on Cliftonville at Solitude. I had only ever been there once before, in April 1970, when the ground was chosen as the neutral venue for the Irish Cup Final between Linfield and Ballymena United. Linfield won two-one, but the match is remembered now mainly for the riot that broke out when fans of both teams clashed with nationalist youths in the streets around the ground. (We were still getting used to the idea in April 1970 that there was no such thing as neutral anymore.) For the next three decades, Cliftonville had been obliged to play many of their 'home' games away, their supporters escorted through the city by almost the entire RUC Reserve.[5]

By 2005, even so solid a working-class Protestant club as Glentoran can go to Solitude once more, although there is still a lot of security, if not yet by the PSNI inside the ground itself. By dint of not being home fans, we have no choice but to sit among the away fans behind one of the goals.

5. The expert on this is Henry McDonald, *Observer* columnist and former member of the Cliftonville 'Red Army'. See *Colours*, his 'exercise in time travel' over the last thirty-odd years of life and politics here.

A quarter of an hour before kick-off a steward comes and motions to my friend to follow him. He leads him down onto the pitch where Glentoran are warming up. He invites him to pose for photographs with his favourite player, striker Andy Smith. On Monday morning he is there on the excellent website: 'Your Man from Japan.'

The match is ninety minutes of anticlimax. In the closing stages Glentoran scramble a winner. Andy Smith doesn't score. It's at the far end of the ground from us, so it is several minutes before the identity of the goal scorer reaches us. I have never heard of him and as I sit here now trying to recall, have quite forgotten him.

A few months later I am in Japan, researching a novel, the point of which is increasingly as much a mystery to me as the Glentoran goalscorer's name. Since I am in the vicinity, that is, within a couple of hundred miles, I go to Beppu to see my friend and to talk to his Junior College English students. These are seventeen- and eighteen-year-olds hoping, at most, to teach high school English. They have no particular interest in Northern Ireland, and no particular reason to learn about it. They just happen to have my friend for a teacher. He has a treat for them, for me: a video of his most recent trip to Belfast. The lights are dimmed, the blinds drawn behind my back on Beppu, and there on the wall before me is the Newtownards Road, there is Connswater Shopping Centre, and there eventually (windscreen in between, blacktop, oncoming traffic) is Solitude. Ten minutes into the action – too strong: *proceedings* – I realize there are no edits. We are in real time, not highlights. Untold minutes later my friend's camera swings around and there I am. Except, I am not there at all, any more than I am at this minute in Beppu. I am three hundred miles away, due east of Belfast, at St James's Park where, a Glentoran fan with a radio has just told me, Manchester United have beaten Newcastle by a goal to nil.

I do not need to watch.

I am not even sure anymore I like to watch.

It is enough to know.

I smile for the camera.

The Yellow Nib, Vol. 3, 2007

A Country for Young Men
(Or Two Quacks and a Son of Dust)

It is not often that you are able to put a precise date on the origins of a novel, but I can be quite specific and say that before 7 April 2006 I had not dreamed of setting a novel in the first decades of the nineteenth century.

At some point during that day, however, I came across 'Belfast Sixty Years Ago: Recollections of a Septuagenarian', a lecture by the Rev Narcissus G. Batt published in the *Ulster Journal of Architecture* in January 1896. Looking back to his boyhood in the 1830s, Rev Batt recalled an inn on the town's northern outskirts rejoicing in the name of the Mill for Grinding Old People Young and run by one Peggy Barclay.

It was the landlady's name, not the inn's, that first attracted me. In the late 1700s, Peggy Barclay had, with her husband James, owned another inn, the Doctor Franklin, in Sugarhouse Entry, just off High Street. It was here, under the quaint and

122

entirely ineffectual disguise of the 'Muddlers' Club' that the Society of United Irishmen met in the years leading up to 1798 and their doomed Rebellion in the name of 'Catholic, Protestant and Dissenter'. Several members of the club, including James Barclay, were betrayed to the British before the rebellion even began by one of the Doctor Franklin's own serving girls, Belle Martin.

To discover Peggy Barclay again, still a landlady, in the early decades of the nineteenth century was not only a delight, but also a reminder that all wars have their post-wars, all risings their settlings. We might not have been able to agree on what to call the events of 1969–1994 in Northern Ireland (the War? the Troubles? the Conflict?) but whatever they were called, there was good reason to hope by April 2006 that we were well beyond them.

My younger daughter was ten weeks old that first week of April, still sleeping in a Moses basket in our bedroom, still waking a couple of times a night, for a feed or a chat. She awoke for the latter on the night of 7 April. I tried to get her to go back to sleep again, holding her in my arms, rocking from foot to foot, and repeating in my head, to keep the rhythm going, 'the Mill for Grinding Old People Young, the Mill for Grinding Old People Young ...' It seemed to inflate like a balloon before my eyes, the novel that I might write, a novel about aftermaths and the accommodations required by the simple passage of time, with, at the heart of it, Peggy Barclay and her inn.

By morning, though, the air had gone out of the balloon entirely. I knew nothing worth the knowing about the early nineteenth century. In the all-important matter of voice, I couldn't begin to 'do' 1830s.

As luck would have it, I had agreed to do a reading that night, 8 April, in Queen's University Belfast, at a conference,

'Cross Currents', organised by postgraduate students from Belfast, Dublin and Aberdeen. I had fully intended coming home straight after the reading (I had not, after all, slept much) but found myself instead, several hours later, with some of the conference's other participants in the Duke of York bar, a bare hundred yards from where the Dr Franklin Tavern had once stood, although Sugarhouse Entry had long ago been downgraded to unmarked alleyway up the side of the Northern Ireland War Memorial Building. I found myself, more to the point, in conversation with Suzanne O'Neill, now a lecturer in the Department of Classics at Trinity College Dublin, then a PhD student at that university, who earlier in the day had delivered a paper called 'From Perikles to Presbyterian "Temples": Liberty, Democracy and Power Architecture in Nineteenth-Century Ulster'.

Suzanne O'Neill had until a short time before no particular interest in nineteenth century Ulster, still less in Presbyterianism. She did, however, have an interest in columns, or, to be precise, in the form of Ionic columns found in the Temple of Apollo Epicurius, built in the fifth century BC at Bassai, in a mountainous area of Arcadia. So remote indeed was the temple that its ruins were only 'discovered' in 1765, by a French archaeologist, who on a return visit to explore the site was murdered by bandits. Ill-luck too befell the next archaeologist to reach the temple, when the ship carrying the sketches he had made was wrecked off the coast of the Peloponnese. An 1812 expedition led by Sir Charles Cockerill had better fortune. The British Museum published detailed drawings of the temple in 1820 and in 1845 Cockerill himself designed the Ashmolean Library in Oxford, incorporating – for the first time since the fifth century BC, it was supposed – the Ionic columns *in antis* particular to Bassai.

In fact, as Suzanne O'Neill had discovered, Cockerill had been beaten to it by a full decade by the architect of – of all things – a Presbyterian Church in – of all places – the Castlereagh hills to the southeast of Belfast.

Bassai it is not, but Castlereagh Presbyterian Church is easily missed today, now that the city has wrapped itself around the foot of the hills, though if you take the trouble to find it (right off the Ring Road, right again, stay in second gear: up) you will understand what a commanding position it once held: commanding enough for the O'Neill family, who ruled this part of Ireland before the Plantation, to have chosen the site for their castle, the so-called 'Eagle's Nest'.

(The story is often told here how, in a later century, the Marquis of Downshire, keen to preserve the castle's ruins, instructed his agent to build a wall around them. The agent passed on the instruction to a mason, who proceeded to build the wall with stones from the ruins he was supposed to be protecting.)

The question Suzanne O'Neill had asked herself, the question that had led her to Cross Currents and thence to the Duke of York, was why that church – with those columns – had been built at that time in that place. The answer, as I understood her, was connected to the fall-out from the 1798 Rebellion, in which Belfast Presbyterians had played so conspicuous a part. In that instant I felt the balloon begin to inflate again. I had an inn in the north of the town, a church in the hills to the southeast; I had, somewhere in the background, by way of a third coordinate, the ghost of 1798.

There still remained the question of voice. I decided to adopt the narrative viewpoint of the essay that had got me started, that of an elderly man looking back from close to the end of the century to the Belfast of his youth. My grandmother, who was still alive, had been born in 1911. Her idiom would have been influenced – inflected – by that of her parents, themselves born in the 1880s. I couldn't do 1830s, but between my great-grandparents and Narcissus G. Batt I thought I could make a stab at, say, 1898, or to take a little pressure off the date, the closing week of the year before that momentous centenary.

I also thought I could try to work the architect of Castlereagh Presbyterian into the plot.

His name was John Millar. His grandfather had a marble yard on Berry Street, off what is now Royal Avenue, one of Belfast's main shopping streets. Then it was Hercules Street, home to forty-nine of the town's eighty-odd butchers, 'an unhealthy and unsavoury area', according to Marcus Patton's *Central Belfast: A Historical Gazetteer*. Millar's father appears for a time to have managed the sandstone quarry at Scrabo, in Newtownards, far enough away from Belfast by the standards of early nineteenth-century travel as to suggest a residence there.

According to Suzanne O'Neill, Millar had been a subscriber to the British Museum publication cataloguing the discoveries at Bassai. Before taking on Castlereagh, he had trained in London with Thomas Hopper, who throughout the 1820s and '30s (and on into the '40s and '50s) was overseeing the building of Gosford Castle at Markethill in County Armagh. Millar's first commission as an architect in his own right was for a pair of villas at Holywood, County Down, on the successful completion of which he entered, and won, the competition for another church, Third Presbyterian, on Rosemary Street, across Hercules Street from Berry Street. That was in 1829 and John Millar was eighteen.

What is remarkable, looking back over a distance of almost two centuries, is that John Millar's precociousness was not at all exceptional. If the past really is another country then Belfast-past was a country for young men. In 1823, a twenty-two-year-old, George Benn, had published (anonymously) a *History of the Town of Belfast, with an accurate account of its former and present state* – for many years after the standard work on the town. With his brother Edward, Benn was also a close associate of the group – several of whom were under twenty – that in 1821 established the Belfast Natural History and Philosophical Society. To begin with, the society met in its members' houses or in the premises of the Linen Hall Library, aka the Belfast Society for Promoting Knowledge, another legacy of the previous century's radical Presbyterianism. By the end of its first decade, however, the society was looking for premises of its own – a museum, no less, where it could display the many curios amassed and discussed by its members.

The building was paid for by public subscription – the first museum to be so funded in all of Ireland – and its design was entrusted to the partnership of Thomas Duff and Thomas Jackson. Jackson was a former pupil of Duff's and Duff, in turn, a pupil of Thomas Hopper's. The Hopper connection might explain why John Millar, called away on who knows what business, shortly after winning the competition for Third Presbyterian, asked Duff and Jackson to oversee the actual construction of his church.

By the time I discovered this I was already well embarked on my novel. It is a fact that once you begin working on any book, you find out all the reasons why it is the very thing that you ought to be writing at that moment. Peggy Barclay had piqued my interest, John Millar had sharpened it, but what finally caused the novel to leap into life was the imaginative connections I had made reading around these two, in particular to the 1831 Port of Belfast Act, which in the development of the town is one of the most important pieces of legislation ever passed.

The passage of the Port Act, indeed, serves as a kind of foundation myth for the modern city of Belfast. Up until then, access to the town by water had been hampered by the tidal River Lagan, which meandered across extensive mudflats to join Belfast Lough. At the lowest tides, water in the docks at the end of High Street dropped to a depth of only three or four feet. Larger vessels had to berth at the Pool of Garmoyle, three miles downriver from the town, where their passengers and cargo were transferred to lighters, or 'gabbards' for the final leg of the journey.

Several plans for 'improvement' had been considered over the years and in the late 1700s a body known as the Ballast Board had been instituted to coordinate and advance these plans. (One early nineteenth-century board member was John McCracken, whose brother Henry Joy McCracken had led the Belfast volunteers in 1798 and had been hanged in the aftermath of their defeat.) The 1831 Act incorporated proposals made by the engineer James Walker for a series of cuts in the course of the Lagan below the town to create a straight channel into the lough. The silt dredged up in the creation of this channel – named, on its completion in 1847, the Victoria Channel – helped to consolidate marshland on the east bank of the river giving rise in time to Queen's Island, which after a few years as a pleasure ground, the 'People's Park', complete with miniature Crystal Palace, became the home of Belfast's most famous shipyard, Harland and Wolff.

That, though, in 1831, was far in the future. The immediate concern for the promoters of the bill was opening up Belfast to overseas markets. No one, it was thought, with the town's best interests at heart could object to a scheme that would benefit all its inhabitants. But objections there were and from the highest echelon of society, Lord Donegall, principal landowner of the town, whose ancestor James Chichester had been granted the town's first charter, by James I, back in 1613.

The Chichesters or their appointees had supplied the town's MPs ever since, returned on a franchise of twelve. They now used their connections at Westminster to harry the bill on its journey through the lower and upper houses. Lord Donegall had struggled for most of his adult life with gambling debts. The prospect – or rather near certainty – of reform threatened his family's continued influence in the town. There is reason to believe that his obstruction was motivated by nothing more than the desire to extract the best price he could for what were still officially his lands.

The lead-up to the act, I had decided, was the ideal backdrop for the novel I had in mind to write and the Ballast Board, or rather the Ballast Office, at the end of High Street, the ideal place of work for my central character, a young man (as recalled by his older self) whom I named Gilbert Rice.

Orphaned at an early age, Gilbert has been raised by his grandfather on Donegall Place (childhood home of Narcissus Batt), a few hundred yards from Berry Street and the marble yard belonging to John Millar's grandfather. Of course he and Millar meet; of course they become friends.

During the early months of 1831, which occupy the bulk of the narrative, Gilbert passes almost daily along Rosemary Street checking on the progress of Third Presbyterian Church, which, insofar as he understands the meaning of the words, looks every bit as 'pure and massive' as his absent friend had intended. When at length Millar himself returns, however, he is appalled by what he finds: this is not the church he designed at all. A single day later and Duff and Jackson would have ruined it utterly. His ire extends to everything that those two 'architects' have touched and when Gilbert tells him, in passing, of the 'time capsule' they have had built into the foundations of the Museum for the benefit and enlightenment of future generations, he is rendered speechless.

The Mill for Grinding Old People Young is a work of fiction; its 'John Millar' is substantially a creature of my own imagination. The historical John Millar left almost nothing in the way of written testimony. Almost. As to the testimony of his architecture, J. B. Doyle, writing in 1854 in *Tours in Ulster*, pronounced Third Presbyterian a 'truly splendid building'. True, its situation, in which Millar had no say, was 'unhappily chosen, the narrow street not permitting its proportions and elevation to be seen to advantage', unlike the building that precedes it in Doyle's tour, the 'very chaste and elegant' museum on the north side of College Square, but all else about it impresses. With its peripteral portico of twenty cast-iron columns (Doric, this time) each weighing two tonnes, it is in fact 'universally admitted to be the most gorgeously finished meeting-house in the kingdom'.

Charles Brett, whose seminal *Buildings of Belfast 1700–1914* was first published in 1966, three years before the start of the Troubles that altered the face of the city forever, remarks in a footnote to Third Presbyterian that Millar emigrated to New Zealand 'shortly after [the church's] completion' – the suggestion is still in high dudgeon at the havoc so nearly wreaked on his plans – but he was certainly in Belfast in 1835 when Castlereagh Presbyterian was completed on the site of the 'Eagle's Nest', and in 1841 when he built another Presbyterian church at Portaferry, once more making use of Ionic Bassai columns. It is more probable that he left Belfast in 1855. His name appears on Christmas Day of that year among the four hundred and thirty passengers on board the *SS Schomberg*, bound from Liverpool to Melbourne, when it ran aground at Peterborough on Australia's 'Shipwreck Coast'. The captain, Forbes, had been below deck playing cards with two women passengers at the time. His ship, built by the Black Ball Line, was considered the 'most perfect clipper ship ever', a curious prefiguring of another maiden-voyage wreck, the White

Star Line's *SS Titanic*, except that all four hundred and thirty of the Schomberg's passengers were picked up unharmed.

John Millar made his way eventually to New Zeland's South Island where he became town engineer for Dunedin. The man who as a twenty-year-old tyro had got the jump on Sir Charles Cockerill and the Ashmolean ended his working life designing street lamps, on which he made sure that his name was embossed.

He died in 1876. Sixty-five years later, on the night of 15/16 April 1941, Third Presbyterian Church was destroyed in a massive German bombing raid on Belfast. Inside one of the portico's columns, a 'time capsule' was found in the form of an engraved slate, the DNA fragment from which I have grown my fictional character:

'POSTERITY know ye that I a son of dust do cause this tablet to be here inserted that you may not attribute the design of this Building to others than myself which I designed in my Eighteenth year and third of my studentship 1829 During an absence from my native Belfast the superintendency was entrusted at its commencement to two quacks Duff and Jackson self-styled architects who so mutilated my designs as to make me almost disown them that portion of the dross you People of refined taste which I can foresee you must be can easily distinguish from the refined on my return I fostered my own child until it grew to what you now behold having begun and finished the Peripteral Portico under my own personal superintendence in the year 1831 JOHN MILLAR ARCHITECT'

The slate can be seen today in Presbyterian Church House, in Fisherwick Place, across the street from Jury's Hotel. A little up the street from Jury's, around the corner into College Square

North, Duff and Jackson's museum building still stands. Until recently the 'Old Museum Arts Centre', it is still the home of the Belfast Natural History and Philosophical Society. And it was there – no longer by anyone's reckoning a young man – that I delivered this lecture in September 2011.

Adapted from lecture to the Belfast Natural History & Philosophical Society, Old Museum, 7 September 2011

Alternative History

The Maharishi arrived by fishing boat in Donaghadee on 13 March 1965 and, being informed of the distance to Bangor, made his way to that town where he checked into Mrs Ivy Kilpatrick's guesthouse on Queen's Parade. The Monarchs showband, who were playing that night in the Royal Ballroom, had a chance encounter with the guru at the door of the chippy next to Barry's amusements and, intrigued by the conversation, returned to Mrs Kilpatrick's the next day in the company of fellow stars of the ballroom circuit, the Gaylords. The guesthouse quickly became a mecca – or rather a *Varanasi* – for showbands, with the Polka Dots, the College Boys and the Fred Hanna's Laganmen all paying court to the Maharishi in the course of the spring. His influence began to be perceived in the bands' sound: from the Boom Boom Rooms in Belfast to the Arcadia in Portrush, raga accordions and atonal banjo drone were the new norm.

It was still, at this stage, very much an underground scene and it was only when members of the Shankill Young Defenders produced tabla drums at that year's Twelfth Demonstration that the wider community began to take notice. The band veered off from the main parade at Stockman's Lane and was rapturously received in its impromptu tour of Andersonstown and Ballymurphy.

An attempted denouncement from the platform at Finaghy Field was met with a sustained *om* from a (predominantly young) section of the Brethren, which spread until the platform party was forced to retract, retreat, and a few days later – the *om* in the meantime having grown deafening – resign.

An enquiry by Minister of Home Affairs, William Craig, found that the Maharishi had paid full board six months in advance, and an attempt by the Royal Ulster Constabulary (RUC) to serve a hastily concocted Extreme Beard Order on him was resisted by an ad hoc alliance of landladies and Saffronists, as the erstwhile Orangemen and their Catholic convert allies now styled themselves.

Unfortunately, before the year was out tensions arose over levitation, both as to its efficacy and – given the local diet of pasty suppers and cream buns – even its possibility. Adherents and opponents – 'Uppers' and 'Downers' – clashed in the street outside Mrs Kilpatrick's in the closing days of August. A subsequent *Sunday Times* 'Insight' report absolved the Maharishi of all responsibility, proving beyond doubt that he was, as he had all along maintained, attending the Ould Lammas Fair in Ballycastle when the violence broke out. Images of people being garrotted with garlands flashed around the world. Not even the release of a single that Christmas ('If Down Was Up and Up Was Down') by the Delta Allstars could arrest the slide towards chaos.

Troops were requested and arrived at Belfast docks on 3 February 1966. That same evening, the Maharishi himself departed, in the company of Mrs Kilpatrick, going out the way he had come a mere eleven months before, travelling the six miles from Bangor to Donaghadee where he boarded a waiting fishing boat.

A cub reporter from the *County Down Spectator*, in Donaghadee to cover the birth of a two-headed lamb, scooped the last interview with him.

'Have you any messages for the people of Northern Ireland?'

'Indeed I have,' said the Maharishi, showing a neat grasp of the vernacular. 'Fuck the whole lot of you.'

Vacuum, April 2012

What They Say You See Is What You Get ...

BBCNI's current affairs strand, *Spotlight*, was this week devoted to the life – and recent death – of 'veteran republican' Martin Meehan. Formerly one of the most active of all the IRA's active service unit members, Meehan in his final years was a Sinn Féin councillor and staunch supporter of Gerry Adams and Martin McGuinness. At the start of this year he spoke, to great effect, at the Extraordinary Ard Fheis called to endorse Sinn Féin support for policing.

Spotlight included footage from earlier programmes in which Meehan had appeared. In one, filmed on the assembly election campaign trail in South Antrim, he was asked by presenter Kevin Magee to account for a device taped to a lamppost beneath an Irish flag, apparently to discourage the flag's removal. He put on his glasses, leaned forward. 'I can't see anything,' he said. You were sure he was going to smile. He didn't.

Last night Belfast's Linen Hall Library hosted the launch of *Walls of Silence* by Catherine McCartney, one of the five sisters of

Robert McCartney murdered in January 2005 by, the sisters have always maintained, members of the 3rd (Belfast) Battalion of the IRA, known locally as the 'Hallion Battalion'. The publication of the book could not be timelier, and not only because, as Catherine says, after initial international outcry, 'the hammer blows against the [republican] wall of silence' over her brother's murder have in recent months been softening, threatening to peter out altogether. At the end of October, Armagh man Paul Quinn was beaten to death in a shed just across the border by a gang of eight men. (Robert McCartney and his friend Brendan Devine were set upon by nine.) His family and friends have laid the blame squarely at the door of the South Armagh IRA. Gerry Adams has denied any republican involvement, suggesting that the murder was the result of a dispute between fuel smugglers. The Irish and British governments indeed made much of his call for those involved to be brought to justice, for anyone with information to go to the police. His comments, however, differ little from the Sinn Féin press statement (quoted by Catherine McCartney) released in the days following the murder of Robert McCartney. McCartney's killing is 'wrong' and 'must be condemned', but is no more than an extension of a growing 'violent knife culture', which must also be condemned. The greater part of the press statement is taken up with condemnation of those seeking to 'score political points' with the 'outrageous claim' of republican involvement and cover-up.

That claim, in fact, originated where the claim of republican involvement in Paul Quinn's murder originated, within the very community that the IRA has passed itself off as protecting all these years. It originated with people who never imagined that they would be in the position of having to speak out against the republican movement and who have been amazed to find themselves, as well as the loved ones they mourn, subject to slur and innuendo.

But while the republican movement's rhetoric might not have changed, there is one big difference between 2005 and 2007: Sinn Féin is now in government. It has not only signed up to policing, but is pressing for the transfer of police and justice powers to a Northern Ireland Executive of which it is the second-largest party. The largest single party, the Democratic Unionists, have been uncharacteristically muted, to say the least, in their response to Paul Quinn's murder, calling for no one to draw any rash conclusions, but to wait instead to see whether there is evidence of 'corporate' IRA responsibility: behind which phrase's Blairite banality lies a volte-face to rival 'four legs good, two legs better'.

Back on Tuesday night's *Spotlight*, meanwhile, Kevin Magee was helpfully pointing out to Martin Meehan the two wires protruding from the package taped to the lamppost. Meehan squinted up at it a while longer, shook his head.

'Your eyesight must be better than mine, Kevin,' he deadpanned.

The disturbing thought is that in the all-new Northern Ireland we are still being asked to believe not what we see but what we are told we should see.

But then, as Catherine McCartney said in the Linen Hall Library, saving 'the Process', it often seems, is more important than saving a life. Except that there is no Process any more, only power and two parties very keen to hold on it, and two governments content to let them.

Guardian, 'Comment Is Free', 22 November 2007

Fundamental Things

We are living, breathing data processors, the world entering us in a continuous present through our orifices and nerve-endings, becoming, in the moment after entry, the past. Most of it disappears almost instantly: anything to do with car keys and cups of coffee, obviously, but huge swathes too of what you might call incidental time. (Pick any five-minute period from earlier in your day, try to relive it second by second, now try it with a five-minute period from yesterday, the day before, this day last year ... Where did it all go?) Memory is what we call a bit of the past that *has* stuck, got broken off and trapped in the brain.

That bit of the past concerns a person who shares your name and a fair bit of your autobiography, but that person is not you. Even with the aid of photographs you would be hard pressed to pick them out in a line-up.

To that extent we do not explore memory so much as try to relate, or to reconcile, all these different people.

A person with my name once broke the aerials off two parked cars while making his way home, drunk, from a university party. A person who has the same birthday as me and occupies the same place in a family of six spent several years in the late eighties and early nineties in Manchester. Another, as a small boy, walked into the living room and saw a woman very like my mother, only younger – younger, younger, younger – sitting in front of the television – nothing like any television now – watching as a man in an LA auditorium asked was there a doctor in the house, while somewhere behind the curtains at his back Bobby Kennedy was dying. Yet another saw his own father stagger in from work, two hours late, and collapse into the same chair, crying over the woman whose body he had picked out of the rubble of the Red Lion Bar on the Ormeau Road, bombed one November 1971 rush-hour by the IRA. The bombers had shouted a ten-second warning. Their bomb went off after six.

Except that can't have been the same chair, or if it was the same chair, it was – three years on from Bobby Kennedy's assassination – in a different house, around the corner and up the hill from the first.

Memory frays at those broken-off edges.

The one thing that memory, in its purest form, should not be confused with, though, is fiction. Fiction – the conscious shaping, manipulation if you prefer, of experience past and present – is the preserve of writers and political parties. I know, I have drawn on the incident of the Red Lion on more than one occasion, and I have heard Sinn Féin saying it never deliberately targeted civilians, just fucked up occasionally, like when a bomb that was supposed to have a ten-second fuse ended up with a fuse four seconds shorter.

Memory tells a different story. Fallible it may be, but cynical never.

The Big Issue, February 2014

Against Closure

Not so long ago the word, on what passes with writers as the street, was that where film and television drama was concerned, at least, the subject of Northern Ireland's recent past was closed. And yet as I speak the clock is ticking down to the UK release of *Hunger*, Steve McQueen's film based on the last weeks of Bobby Sands's fast to the death. As I speak too a biopic of Bernadette McAliskey — Devlin as was — is in production and another of the Reverend Ian Paisley is being mooted. I confess this sudden revival of interest baffled as much as delighted me until I read an interview with a leading southern Irish director who said that the series that *he* was planning to set in the North would hammer six-inch nails into the coffin of the conflict, quote 'so that that particular vampire never came out again'. And then it clicked. Recent political developments here are supposed to have ended the story once and for all. No fear now of another twist in the tale, of events conspiring to bite a putative director in the bum ... or neck.

Forget for a moment that the story was supposed to have ended back in the 1990s at the time of the first IRA ceasefire; this rush to nail down the lid is just the other side of the subject-already-closed coin.

I try to imagine what would happen if the same attitude was adopted towards other places and times. In successive days this summer I finished Philip Roth's *The Plot Against America*, which imagines a USA under Charles Lindbergh cosying up to Hitler's Germany, and watched Stefan Ruzowitzky's Oscar-winning film *The Counterfeiters*, based on the experiences of concentration camp survivor, and forger, Adolf Burger. Just this week I finally caught up with the film version of Ian McEwan's *Atonement*: the Dunkirk Evacuation and all that. It didn't do for me what *The Counterfeiters* did, or indeed McEwan's own novel, but my cultural life – I hesitate before the word 'nation's' – would have been the poorer without it.

When it comes to history and art there is, or ought to be, no statute of limitations: that's anyone's history, anyone's art. So forgive me if when next I hear the word *closure* I itch to reach again for my *qwerty* crowbar.

Free Thought, Radio 3, 20 August 2008

Against Closure II
(On the Reopening of Ormeau Library)

It says much about how things have changed in Belfast that sometimes there are just more things on in a week, or even a night, than you can possibly get to. One of my big regrets of recent weeks is that I was unable to get to the Lyric Theatre to hear the Israeli writer David Grossman being interviewed, although the mere fact of his coming here has sent me back to his books, fiction and non-fiction.

In particular I have been reading his essays on literature and politics published, by Bloomsbury, as *Writing in the Dark*. The title essay takes as its starting point Franz Kafka's 'A Little Fable', a story so short it is easier to tell in its entirety than explain:

'Alas,' said the mouse, 'the whole world is growing smaller every day. At the beginning it was so big that

I was afraid, I kept running and running, and I was glad when I saw walls far away to the right and left, but these long walls have narrowed so quickly that I am in the last chamber already, and there in the corner stands the trap that I must run into.' 'You only need to change your direction,' said the cat and ate it up.

Writing in 2007, the year after his younger son was killed in the Israeli invasion of Lebanon, Grossman talks of the 'shrinking of our soul's surface' in times of conflict. Not only does the world get smaller, so too 'does the language that describes it'. Complexities and subtleties are replaced by clichés and slogans.

'The more hopeless the situation seems,' he says, 'and the shallower the language becomes, the more the public discourse dwindles.'

It is against this backdrop that he writes. Nine out of the essay's last fifteen paragraphs, indeed, begin with the words 'I write':

'I write and the world does not close in on me.'

'I write. I feel the many possibilities that exist in every human situation.'

And, most beautifully, 'I write, and I feel that the correct and accurate use of words acts like a medicine. It purifies the air I breathe, removes the pollutants, and frustrates the schemes of the language defrauders.'

And as I read what he writes I feel the same purification.

Reading has that capacity to return the world to us afresh.

I was reminded of David Grossman's 'language defrauders' recently when I was reading another book, *Whoops!*, John Lanchester's brilliant analysis of the financial crisis, subtitled 'Why everyone owes everyone and no one can pay.'

At one point Lanchester makes a distinction between 'industry' and 'business'. It is not just a lexical difference, but a cultural difference, even an anthropological one.

'An industry is an entity which as its primary purpose makes or does something, and makes money as a by-product. The car industry makes cars, the television industry makes TV programmes, the publishing industry makes books, and with a bit of luck they all make money too ... Most human enterprises, especially the most worthwhile and meaningful ones, are in that sense industries, focused primarily on doing what they do: healthcare and education are both, from this anthropological perspective, industries.'

So too, he might have added, are libraries.

The purpose of a business on the other hand is 'purely and simply to make money.'

Since the deregulation of the City in the 1980s – Margaret Thatcher's 'Big Bang' – business – money – has been in conflict with industry, with every human enterprise that is not primarily concerned with making more money. The language of business has infiltrated – I would say polluted – all areas of life, shrinking the surface of our souls.

A library should not have to make a business argument. A library is its own argument.

Secular and non-commercial, libraries are public spaces that privilege learning and contemplation.

I think again of the purification of which David Grossman writes. William Pitt famously said that the parks were the lungs of London. Libraries provide similar ventilation for the imagination. How apt that the entrance to this wonderful new library should be facing the gates of Ormeau Park.

In this age of austerity our public institutions are under threat as never before. There has been a retreat – sometimes forced, sometimes willingly undertaken – into the private sphere. An increasing number of us it seems would rather go online to search for the information we need than go up the street to a library. Yet the Internet, which seemed to offer unlimited access to knowledge, appears increasingly trammelled by advertising and government scrutiny. Choice is being narrowed, not broadened.

Libraries these days do many things, but first and foremost they do books.

Libraries are as old as the written word. They have outlived all the ideologies that human beings have invented to organise their lives by, and control the lives of others, even those ideologies that were so threatened by libraries that they tore them down and burnt the books they housed.

Libraries, I am sure, with vigilance on all our parts, will outlive this present ideological obsession with business and money.

This particular library, I am sure, will outlive me, and serve generations yet to come, helping to remove some of the pollutants from their culture.

David Grossman concludes 'Writing in the dark' not with 'I write,' but 'we write': 'We write. How fortunate we are. The world does not close in on us. The world does not grow smaller.'

How fortunate we are that libraries allow us the opportunity to read, that they stop the world from closing in on us, from growing smaller.

20 June 2012

Wonders

A strange thing happened to me one night last autumn as I strolled through Belfast's Cathedral Quarter.

No, really: strolled.

A policeman stopped me, or at least a person dressed as a policeman stopped me. 'If you wouldn't mind waiting a minute,' he said. 'We're filming.'

'Be my guest,' I said and went and stood with a dozen or so other night-time strollers who had invited him to be their guest too.

'Bollywood,' one of them said to me.

'I beg your pardon?'

'The film, it's a Bollywood.'

I looked more closely. He was right.

And the strangest thing? Neither of us were the least surprised.

Time was and not so long ago the only cameras on our streets belonged to news crews. I have a vivid childhood memory (sorry, did I say 'not so long ago?') of finding one Swedish crew wandering the grounds of my primary school, lost and forlorn. It was my first exposure to brushed denim. The horror has not yet left me.

Belfast still has the capacity to attract the attention of international reporters, but more and more it is attracting the attention of international filmmakers. A few weeks after that Bollywood night, Ridley Scott announced he would be making six low-budget features here over the next three years.

Our greatest coup, however, was attracting the American HBO channel to the city to film *Game of Thrones*.

The artist Bill Drummond (formerly of the KLF), discovering that Belfast had no twin city, once attached a sign below the 'Welcome to Belfast' that greets you as you enter from the south by the MI motorway: 'Twinned with your wildest dreams,' it read. Now, even in your wildest dreams, you might think, Belfast would struggle to double as the fantasyland of Westeros, but – every cloud its silver lining – the demise of shipbuilding here happened to leave vacant a giant paint hall, the size of several film studios, on the opposite side of the River Lagan from the city centre, in what was once Harland and Wolff and is now the Titanic Quarter.

Even before *Game of Thrones* hit town this 'Paint Hall Studio' had done service as the underground 'City of Ember' in Gil Kennan's 2008 movie of that name, starring Tom Cruise, and – encouragingly – co-starring a number of Northern Irish actors.

Time was, and a lot more recently than the days of disoriented Swedish camera crews, if you wanted to work in film you had to move elsewhere. If you wanted to make a film *set in* Belfast you had to go to Dublin or Liverpool to film it. Now, not only actors, but artists like the composer and producer David Holmes, with more than twenty soundtracks to his credit, can carry on an international career and work on films generated by – and filmed in – the city itself.

If you are not currently connected to a suitable device, by the way, I suggest that as soon as is practicable you listen to 'I Heard Wonders' from Holmes's 2009 *Holy Pictures* album, preferably while standing on Belfast's Queen's Bridge, the city centre to the left of you, the Titanic Quarter to the right, ahead of you the Lagan opening into Belfast Lough.

Wildest dreams?

Just be sure to wear something tight to keep your heart from bursting.

British Airways *High Life*, December 2012

26.5 Million Into 1

'All wars are full of stories that sound like fiction'
— Javier Cercas, *Soldiers of Salamis*

At eight o'clock on the night of Monday, 20 December 2004, a young couple out Christmas shopping in Belfast noticed something odd about the occupants of the white van parked in Wellington Street, close to the City Hall: they were wearing ginger wigs beneath their baseball caps. The couple alerted a traffic warden, who contacted police. Two officers were dispatched, but by the time they arrived the van was gone.

At eleven o'clock a 999 call was made from a house in Poleglass, in west Belfast. The caller, twenty-three-year-old Chris Ward, said he worked as a supervisor at the cash centre of the Northern Bank in Wellington Street. For the past twenty-four hours a gang had been holding hostage his entire family and the wife of the cash centre's assistant manager, Kevin McMullan.

Earlier that evening this gang had forced him to carry one million pounds out of the bank in a Glasgow Celtic sports bag and give it to a man at a bus stop on Queen Street. The operator interrupted: 'And then you went home?' she said, somewhat optimistically. 'No,' said Chris Ward. 'That was just the start of it.' The gang returned, twice, in a white van and loaded it up with another £25.5 million in new and used notes.

It was at the time the biggest bank robbery in the history of these islands.

From the outset the evidence seemed to point to the Provisional IRA: the sheer scale of the operation, involving up to thirty men, the fact that one of the houses taken over – the Wards' – was in an area where the Provisionals traditionally held sway, the similarities with other robberies attributed to the IRA by the Independent Monitoring Commission on paramilitary activity.

Just over a month later, Robert McCartney was murdered outside a Belfast bar. Again, despite Sinn Féin denials, the IRA was blamed. For a time, British and Irish ministers spoke with unusual candour (and anger) about the symbiotic relationship between the political and military wings of republicanism; newspapers ran stories on money-laundering operations stretching deep into Eastern Europe, investment portfolios running into the scores, possibly even hundreds of millions.

Finally, in July, after half a year of cold shoulders and bad press, the IRA announced it had decommissioned its remaining weapons, which had a pleasing circularity about it. Such was the volume of phone traffic between senior republicans ahead of the Northern job that the security services monitoring it had fondly imagined decommissioning was going to occur then: an early Christmas present from the Boys.

Chris Ward, meantime, had been feeling pressure of his own. Less than a month after the robbery he had granted BBC

Northern Ireland's *Spotlight* programme an unprecedented interview in which he addressed the whispering campaign against him. He was a young Catholic man from west Belfast, he was assistant treasurer of his local Glasgow Celtic Supporters' Club, his ex-girlfriend, another Northern Bank employee, was the daughter of a well-known republican. In some people's eyes, he said, that was enough to make him guilty of involvement.

It hadn't occurred to me until that moment that he might have been involved, but this turning of the tables on his accusers, accusing them rather of bigotry, seemed to play so cleverly on the sensitivities of our times that I said to my wife the moment the interview ended, 'My God, it *was* him.'

On 29 November 2005 police arrested Chris Ward and, having applied for three extensions to the detention period, holding him longer than any suspect in British legal history, charged him shortly after midnight on 7 December with armed robbery and kidnapping.

Earlier this year a friend who works at the BBC in Belfast phoned me, asking if I would be interested in working with her on a film about the robbery and the forthcoming trial.

We were agreed that our way in would be that extraordinary *Spotlight* interview. We would cut between that and the police interrogation, between both of those and the courtroom, where, we were pretty sure from what we had heard (not least the fact that the prosecution's star witness was to be Kevin McMullan), Chris Ward would be found guilty.

Besides, the Public Prosecution Service had recently lost two high-profile cases, against Sean Hoey, over the 1998 Omagh bomb, and Terence Davison, accused of murdering Robert McCartney. It would surely not risk further embarrassment by bringing another case it was not confident of winning; and if it was in any doubt it would surely, surely, *surely* not be appointing the same barrister, Gordon Kerr QC, as had presided over the two earlier defeats. Would it?

Due to other work commitments I couldn't attend the first week of the trial, which opened in Court Number 11 of Belfast's Laganside Courts on 9 September. I turned up instead at the beginning of the second week, having been led to believe that Kevin McMullan would be taking the stand.

The first thing I saw on stepping out of the lift on the fourth floor (Crown Courts) was a phalanx of police officers, clad in 'riot-lite', their presence reflecting for me the gravity of an offence that had almost succeeded in derailing the entire peace process. Not until I had pushed – no, *negotiated* – my way through them to the door they were guarding did I realize I had got the wrong courtroom. This was Number 13, where five members of the Notarantonio family from Ballymurphy, also in west Belfast, were appearing on charges arising from a feud with a family called Devlin.

Twenty-one-year-old Francisco Notarantonio, accused of the manslaughter of Gerard Devlin, was the namesake of his grandfather, murdered by the Ulster Freedom Fighters (UFF) in 1987. It was later alleged that the elder Francisco Notarantonio had been offered up to the UFF to protect another west Belfast man of Italian descent, Freddie Scappaticci, codenamed Stakeknife, one of British Intelligence's most valuable agents inside the IRA. (Rumours still abound of an even more valuable agent: Martin McGuinness, codename the Fisherman.) The Ballymurphy feud appeared to have political undertones: another grandson, Joseph O'Connor, a member of the dissident Real IRA, was murdered in the estate in October 2000, almost certainly by the Provisionals.

Retracing my steps along the fourth-floor corridor, I passed Court Number 12, in which the trial was due to begin of Michael Stone, the loyalist killer who served a Northern

Irish life (twelve years of the thirty minimum to which he was sentenced) for the murders of three mourners at an IRA funeral in 1988. On his release from prison, under the terms of the Good Friday Agreement, Stone had reinvented himself as a painter – a surprisingly popular one – and a commentator on his own past, appearing in BBC2's *Facing the Truth* alongside Archbishop Desmond Tutu (Stone gave him a painting) and the wife of a man Stone had claimed to have murdered. (Stone changed his story on the night: 'facing the truth of his former lie' was clearly a comfort to him, though not to the murdered man's wife, who left the studio in tears.) In November 2006 Stone was on television again, trapped by alert security guards in the revolving door of the parliament building at Stormont, brandishing what turned out to be an imitation pistol, but with a very authentic knife and a wire garrotte about his person: to kill Sinn Féin politicians, according to the prosecution; as props in a performance art piece, according to his defence.

Court 11 was at the far end of the corridor. A vending machine stood facing the entrance, stocked with crisps and drinks and a selection of chocolate bars. Inside, the courtroom had an art house feel, its meagre audience consisting of the defendant's parents and no-longer-ex girlfriend and a couple of representatives of the Northern Bank. With the exception of the court reporter, who preferred the press benches, the handful of journalists present spread themselves out across the jury benches opposite, it having been decided that this was one of those exceptional cases that can still be tried here without a jury. Such cases are generally understood to be terrorist-related, but not only was Chris Ward sitting alone in a dock that could have held the thirty-strong gang in comfort, there didn't appear to be much interest in establishing the identity of the absent parties. The judge, Mr Justice McLaughlin, was explicit: 'We are not here to decide whether the people who did this came from an organisation or a criminal gang or both.' Absent too, therefore, was any reference to motive, or for that matter to the whereabouts of the proceeds.

The evidence to be presented was, I read in Gordon Kerr's opening statement, 'circumstantial', which meant it would not include the audio tapes from the Ward home – bugged by the security services after charges had been brought – or from the Spanish apartment to which Chris Ward went the spring after the robbery with his supposedly still-estranged girlfriend.

The journalists I talked to each had their particular theory as to why the tapes weren't being used. One told me that Chris Ward was heard on them to say, 'I'm scared if I talk to the cops those fuckers will come back and shoot me in the head', which, the journalist suggested, was either the performance of someone schooled in counter-surveillance, or the outburst of a genuinely terrified young man. Another was convinced political pressure had been applied to prevent the revelation that, as the phone traffic implied, very senior republicans were involved in the robbery. Except he didn't say very senior republicans, he said Bobby Storey and Bik (born Brendan) McFarlane.

Bobby Storey, most commentators agree, is the IRA's director of intelligence, a staunch Adams-McGuinness loyalist. As early as 11 January 2005, the MP for South Antrim, David Burnside, named him under parliamentary privilege as having masterminded the robbery. In 1983 Storey had planned and executed a mass escape from the Maze Prison, along with the IRA's Officer Commanding in the jail, Bik McFarlane, who at the time was doing life for the murders of three men and two women in a bomb attack on the Bayardo Bar on Belfast's Shankill Road.

In his book *Ripe for the Picking: The Inside Story of the Northern Bank* (Gill & MacMillan, 2006), Chris Moore repeatedly draws comparisons between the tactics of the Maze escapers and the

Northern Bank robbers. McFarlane, for instance, asked one evidently devout family whose farmhouse he had taken over in the aftermath of the escape to swear on the Bible that they would not alert the authorities for seventy-two hours after he and his comrades left. Likewise, the Ward family were asked to swear on a holy picture that they would not do anything contrary to the robbers' commands.

(It was a central plank of the prosecution case that the gang had been more lenient with the Wards than the McMullans, allowing family members to go unaccompanied to their rooms and even watch DVDs: *Shanghai Nights* and *Pirates of the Caribbean.*)

There was no sign of Kevin McMullan at all that first day I was in court, or for the rest of that week indeed, which was taken up with the screening of police interviews with Chris Ward in the immediate aftermath of the robbery, while he was still officially a victim and a witness. I found myself torn between watching the videos and watching Chris Ward in the dock, watching himself. He had put on weight around his face and neck since those interviews, one of those changes in body shape that later prove to be definitive: his father, visible over his left shoulder, was recognisably the man Chris would become. Back in 2004, he was by his own account to the police, a 'wee man', literally – five foot eight, size six Caterpillar boot – and metaphorically: 'I'm not important … I'm just a guy who carries keys.' This self-deprecating vein ran right through the interviews. He was 'a bit of a bore' compared to other guys his age, who were usually out in clubs. All he really cared about was Celtic, although when it came to watching football he wasn't choosy: 'If eleven bottles of 7-Up were playing eleven bottles of 7-Up I'd watch it.'

If he was a bore he had an engaging way of saying it. Here was someone, I thought as I listened, who liked to talk, who even in the most innocent circumstances might say a little more than he had intended, out of common courtesy, a duty to keep the conversation going. In this too he reminded me of his father, who as the week went on I saw in the corridor between sessions, or out in the streets round about, looking for lunch, and who always spoke to me, to anyone connected with the trial, prosecution or defence, journalist or cop; like I knew, in the same situation, my own father would.

The judge wasn't quite so diverted by the interviews. 'Is there anything I'm supposed to be on the lookout for here?' he asked, having called for a pause midway through the second day. 'Keep me alert. It's about the most boring video I've ever watched.'

The prosecution contended that there were contradictions and omissions in these interviews, especially in relation to the preparation of the staff rota, which had paired the defendant and Kevin McMullan as dual key-holders to the Cash Centre on that fateful Monday in December 2004. Chris Ward himself had drawn up the rota.

Reluctantly ('None of this can be fast-forwarded or anything of that nature?'), Mr Justice McLaughlin ordered the play button be pressed again.

Later, as I was walking to the lift, a junior barrister, recognising which court I had come out of, called to me. 'How's the show trial? Bouncing up and down on his bed in a Celtic shirt, shouting up the Provos, he must be guilty!'

I laughed, but still I felt a little sheepish. Up close and away from all the pre-trial speculation, the case had begun to take on a very different aspect, with inference and interpretation taking the place of hard evidence. When the court wound up for the weekend I talked to my friend from the BBC.

'If we're depending on a guilty verdict then I don't think we've got a film,' I said. 'I mean if I was sitting where I'm sitting as a *juror* I wouldn't convict on what I've heard.'

All the same, on Monday morning I headed off to the court again. I arrived twenty minutes early for the morning session (I had a book with me: *Soldiers of Salamis*), so was present when a court official came in and laid a hank of Kleenex in the witness box beside the customary jug of water. At eleven o'clock exactly Mr Justice McLaughlin made his entrance and Kyran, not Kevin, McMullan took the stand.

My first impression was that she had carried into her early thirties much of the woman she had become in her teens, a sports player, maybe (camogie, as it turns out: women's hurling). From the moment she started to speak, however, it was clear that the events of 19–20 December 2004 had divided her life into two unequal parts: before and after. She didn't so much recount the kidnapping as relive it. After mentioning the black plastic ties with which her hands were bound, she remained for some moments staring at her wrists. She described, as though it were there before her, the gun carried by the gang's leader ('of an age, and used, with a mark down the barrel') and came back for a second go at the knife dangled in front of her face while she lay trussed on the floor. Not a kitchen knife, 'This was something vicious, I don't know what purpose they're made for.' More vivid and harrowing still was the moment when she learned she was to be separated from her husband and taken, as she believed, to a house where there would be a woman gang member to care for her. Her eyes were to be sealed shut with Sellotape for the journey. Terrified, Kyran persuaded her kidnappers to allow her to put on a hat, which they could pull down over her eyes. As soon as the hat was in place, however, the tape came out anyway, wound round and round and round her head … When her voice failed her hands took over, violently performing the action: round and round and round; then she broke down altogether.

The judge suggested an early lunch.

Out in the corridor I met the junior barrister who had shouted 'show trial' the week before. Today he suggested I take a look into Court Number 12, which was still in session, and in which Michael Stone was currently giving evidence.

'In mime?' I asked.

Mime, though, would have been marginally less bizarre. Stone was hunched forward in the witness box when I went in, addressing the counsel for defence, Orlando Pownell QC, in the same measured voice with which he had addressed Archbishop Desmond Tutu and the wife of the man he remembered he had not killed, fifteen years after confessing to his murder.

From what I could gather, he was explaining how, ahead of his attempt on Stormont, he had requested a camera crew from ITN, had even suggested to them some cutaways and 'looking shots'. This was, we were to understand, an artistic plot rather than a criminal one. His performance consisted of him playing the part of a dissident loyalist in order to 'destroy the iconography' of Michael Stone, dissident loyalist hero.

Later he would deconstruct item by item his apparel and accessories on the day in question. The wire was not a garrotte but a reference to the painting he gave Desmond Tutu, a symbol of the fragile path to peace and reconciliation; his fisherman's hat was a pretty literal nod to those rumours (the certain fact, to Stone) of Martin McGuinness's role as a British agent; the thirty pounds in his pocket represented the thirty pieces of silver and the betrayal of the peace process by Sinn Féin and the DUP – and so on. The whole ensemble amounted to a 'comic parody' of his former self. 'I would rather be remembered as an eccentric artist that got it wrong in performance art than for my past, when I did some terrible things.'

In Court Number 11 after the recess Kyran McMullan continued the account of the terrible things done to her by the Northern Bank robbers.

Despite the assurances, there was no woman at the second house she was taken to, just two other men and the man who had earlier dangled the vicious-looking knife in front of her. There was a bed, but blindfolded as she was (blindfolded? mummified almost) she was afraid to lie down on it lest she be raped. She feared even the offer of tea: 'It takes so much trust,' she said, 'to take something from someone you can't see.'

Then, almost twenty-four hours into the ordeal, she was made to strip to her underwear and put on a boiler suit, before being led out to a car. Here the knife-man, on whom she had come perversely to depend, tried to take off her hat: to destroy the forensics, he said. She fought to keep it on, certain that its removal – and her seeing him – was the excuse he needed to kill her. When, inevitably, the hat was yanked off she kept her eyes squeezed shut, long after he had pushed her face down on to the car seat. She was driven to a clearing in a wood and ordered to lie flat on the ground for ten minutes.

'I was waiting for the bullet in the back of the head,' she said. Still, she tried, despite her terror, to count off the minutes. Halfway through she heard a *whumph* behind her.

'I thought it was a car burning, and that made sense. They'd burn the car they'd been driving me about in.' She paused while she summoned her contempt. 'Because that's what they do in this country.'

It got to the point in the clearing when she had no option but to stand – 'That's ten!' she shouted. It was late December; she was wearing only a boiler suit. Her body temperature had dropped dangerously low.

'I never felt cold like it,' she said. Never in the life *before*, I took her to mean, for she looked at that moment as though she would never in the life after be able to shake it.

By a quirk of scheduling, BBCNI was screening a film that same night to mark the twenty-fifth anniversary of the 1983

Maze escape. *Breakout* is the kind of film that would have been unthinkable even five years ago. Gerry Kelly, now Sinn Féin's spokesperson on justice and policing, spoke candidly about shooting a prison officer in the head (the officer survived, unlike a colleague, James Ferris, who died of a heart attack after being stabbed) and generally gave a good account, from the perpetrator's side, of the kind of violence and threat of violence that had been visited on Kyran and Kevin McMullan. In this account he was aided by fellow escapers Bobby Storey and Bik McFarlane. Storey, whose official title was given as Head of Sinn Féin in Belfast, spoke in the pseudo-military jargon preferred by Michael Stone in his television (and court) appearances. He didn't, though, seem to share Stone's interest in destroying his own iconography: he now gives lectures on the escape to invited audiences. (Cameras not permitted. The language there, I am told, is a little less military, a little more gloating.)

The morning after *Breakout* was screened, counsel for Chris Ward, Arthur Harvey, told Kyran McMullan he did not intend to put her through the further ordeal of cross-examination. Instead he reserved his not inconsiderable inquisitorial powers for her husband, who took the stand directly after his wife stood down. Having pointed to inconsistencies in Kevin McMullan's own version of events, Harvey successfully challenged the reliability of the assistant manager's memory on every point of divergence with Chris Ward's story. The all-important rota, which Chris Ward was supposed to have manipulated to the robbers' advantage, was portrayed as an ad hoc, constantly evolving arrangement. Kevin McMullan himself had contributed to the circumstances leading to him and Chris Ward being paired together on Monday, 20 December, by asking to leave early on the previous Friday. 'An emergency,' he had said. To get a present for Kyran, he admitted to Harvey. A jumper, from Next.

The final witness to take the stand was the Cash Centre's manager, Maria Redmond. She seemed, briefly, to raise the possibility that there was still some mileage in the rota, but having been persuaded to accept Arthur Harvey's assessment of her as a 'people person' and 'a good judge of character', she accepted too his judgement of Chris Ward: 'An open young man?' 'Yes.' 'Likeable?' 'Yes.' 'An honest and reliable worker?' 'Yes.'

And with that the case was pretty much over.

There were a few more adjournments and times for reflection before Gordon Kerr rose to his feet on the morning of 9 October and declared, with a good grace, that in the light of the evidence presented since the beginning of the trial the test for prosecution could no longer be met.

Given this decision to present no further evidence, Mr Justice McLaughlin told the court that he could arrive at no other verdict than that Chris Ward was not guilty of all charges.

Whereupon Chris Ward said the only two words he had spoken since the beginning of the trial.

'Thank you.'

A little later, on the pavement outside the court, his solicitor, Niall Murphy, read a statement, which returned to his client's theme in that *Spotlight* interview back in January 2005.'[I]t is a regrettable fact that in this society the mere fact that Chris Ward was a Catholic from Poleglass and charged with this offence was enough to seal his guilt in the eyes of some people.'

It was not the time, or the place, to interject that that was not quite how it was for me and, frankly, I wondered if I wasn't protesting – or wanting to protest – too much. It was very simple, Chris Ward was the one person in Belfast who had been proven in a court of law to have had no involvement whatever in the robbery of £26.5 million from the Northern Bank.

I did manage to locate his father in the corridor by the vending machine, struggling, in his emotion, to send a text. I shook his hand, told him I was delighted for him. And I was. Am.

Chris Ward turned twenty-six the Sunday after he was acquitted. That same day the *Sunday Independent* published a claim that IRA investments in the New York financial markets (some $250 million) had been 'devastated' by the crash and that well-known republican figures in Belfast were in 'a state of panic' over the losses.

Who knows what the security services made of all that phone traffic.

A week later came the news that the prosecution team in the Omagh bomb trial, led by Gordon Kerr, had earned £1.2 million, or slightly more than could fit into a Celtic holdall. The fees for the Northern Bank have yet to be calculated. At time of writing too it is unclear whether the judge in the Michael Stone trial will accept the defendant's claim that he was *playing* rather than *being* himself when he tried to force his way into Stormont.[1]

Bobby Storey is still giving his Maze escape lectures.

Bik McFarlane can be found on YouTube performing 'Song for Marcella' (Bobby Sands's prison nickname) and 'Something Inside so Strong'.

Maybe twenty-odd years from now there'll be a video there too explaining who really robbed the Northern Bank and subjected the McMullans and the Wards to the trauma they suffered in December 2004.

Notes towards a screenplay, November 2008

---

1. He didn't.

The End of Surprise

They're raising the Titanic idea again. It's the front-page story in one of our morning papers. Seems the government — the one we actually voted for ourselves, as opposed to the one the people of Bedford voted for, or against — is considering a plan to build a 'boat-shaped extension' to the Odyssey Arena, home, appropriately enough, to the Giants, Belfast's ice hockey team, in time for the great liner's/iceberg magnet's centenary celebrations in 2012. Unlike previous plans, however (the floating restaurant of 1995 springs to mind ... sank without trace), this one might just come to pass. There is a new spirit of optimism here, a belief that because we did finally form a government without the help of the people of Bedford (though you were bricks in the past, People of Bedford, absolute bricks), we can do whatever we put our mind to. Even something as crass as bolting a four-funnelled hotel and conference centre on to the back of an ice hockey arena.

164

Francis Fukuyama famously declared that the fall of the Berlin Wall signalled the end of history. Given what the world has served up for future historians in the twenty years since, no one would be stupid enough (you would think) to declare our recent Peace Process the end even of history's little Northern Irish subplot. No, if we are living at the end of anything here it is *surprise*. Ian Paisley and Martin McGuinness set the tone, arch enemies who not so much embraced in government as carried on a public year-long pash, before Paisley retired and McGuinness made him a parting gift of two handwritten poems, one by Seamus Heaney the other by Martin himself. (He's fond of poetry, our Deputy First Minister, although obviously decommissioning has put Browning beyond his reach.)

Set against this the fact that, a decade and a half after the last explosion was heard on its streets, Belfast has finally been knocked off-centre by so mundane a thing as a shopping precinct scarcely causes an eyebrow to flicker. Mind you 'precinct' doesn't really do justice to Victoria Square, which opened to great fanfare this spring. With its ninety-eight shops (a third of the previous total for the entire city), restaurants, cinemas and 100-plus apartments, Victoria Square is closer to a town within a town; it even has a thirty-five-metre diameter dome mirroring (literally: it's made of glass) the one on top of the City Hall, which for the past century has stared grandly down Donegall Place and Royal Avenue, Belfast's main shopping streets. Former main shopping streets, I should maybe say. Since spring 'relocated' and 'to let' signs have appeared in more than one shop window along their quarter-mile stretch.

Wandering around Victoria Square, meantime, I am reminded of the account of Belfast at the beginning of the nineteenth century after the failed United Irishmen's rebellion: 'A strange apathy fell on the politically minded in the North while ... a wild and extravagant gaiety dominated the scene'.

(Maybe some Fukuyama was peddling the end of history line then, too.) Actually wandering around it the first time I was completely disoriented: *Where was my Belfast?*

It is in the nature of cities, however, and not just of the times, that nothing stays strange for too long and whether intentionally or not what the architects of Victoria Square have in fact done is give us fresh angles on this particular city.

In the bad old Browning-and-car-bomb days there were security barriers and gates around this part of town, which might explain why I never noticed Upper Church Lane before, much less walked along it as I can do now, on to Church Lane itself and then, cutting across High Street, straight down Skipper Street, and on, irresistibly, to Hill Street, past some of the city's best new bars (Muriel's, the Spaniard – think wild, think extravagant, think slightly above average gaiety) as well as the ghosts of some important old ones: it was in a tavern down an entry behind Skipper Street that those United Irishmen first met, while more recently 10 Hill Street was the Harp, a strippers' bar taken over in the 1970s by Belfast's punks.

Punk was officially a latecomer to Belfast but it tapped into something that had long existed in our local brand of rock 'n' roll. (Two words: Them, 'Gloria'.) A musician friend who saw Snow Patrol in Australia said he knew straightaway where they were from: 'With southern bands the default setting is folk, with northern bands it's punk.'

Gary Lightbody, as it happens, has an office just off Hill Street, or at least has a desk in a dusty room in the former whiskey warehouse now known as the Oh Yeah Project, which offers rehearsal spaces, and then some, to the latest crop of thrilling Belfast bands (two more words: Panama Kings).

The month before Victoria Square opened, Oh Yeah hosted an after party for Terri Hooley, who had just received a lifetime achievement award for services to the Northern Irish music industry. Terri (there might be people alive who still haven't heard him tell the story) famously released the Undertones' 'Teenage Kicks' on his own Good Vibrations label, named after the record shop he opened in 1978 when nobody was opening anything in Northern Ireland. Within four years he was bankrupt, but not before his shop had entered into the city's folk (*punk*) lore. Other shops followed, and inevitably folded. The latest opened at the end of June in Winetavern Street behind our last great-white-retail-hope, the Castlecourt Centre.

Recently I came across a magazine article from 1970 in which Terri, then a twenty-year-old poetry magazine editor and leader of a 'tribe' of hippies, proclaimed, 'Every man has the right to live his own life without fear from the police, Protestants, Catholics or whoever, and we'll give up everything, our lives, to this end. We're ready now!'

Even at the End of Surprise it's a wonder that it took the likes of Paisley and McGuinness forty years to catch on to his politics, and his poetry. Here's hoping that amid the fake funnels and glass domes Belfast hangs on too to his rock 'n' roll soul.

GQ Style, August 2008

Remember the First Time

I had spent Monday night at a concert called 'Do You Remember the First Time' in the refurbished Ulster Hall: a dozen Northern Irish bands playing one of their own songs and one from a gig they had attended there in the past. The friend giving me a lift home told me the moment I got into her car that a policeman had been murdered in Lurgan. (She had picked it up, not as she once might have done on the shortwave police radio, but on her Blackberry.) The next morning another friend, an American, who had been at the concert emailed to say how awful it was to hear what had happened while we were singing our heads off. In fact that's what it was like growing up here: great nights out rounded off with sobering news. For too many people, of course, their night out became the news.

I remember, the first time I was allowed to stay over at a primary-school friend's house, hearing the shots that killed two policemen at our local shops. Like most of my fellow citizens over the age of thirty, I have been remembering a great deal else in the past few days.

I had got into the habit of telling people that we in Northern Ireland were living not at the end of history but of surprise: so many highs and lows since the Good Friday Agreement, and yet I was floored by the news from Lurgan and from Antrim two nights before. And not even in my most anxious moments – because the recent attacks did not come entirely out of the blue – did I imagine that I would find myself again, as I found myself this afternoon, at another peace rally outside Belfast City Hall. How many of those *were* we at down the years? A time-lapse montage, I suspect, would show many of the same faces, growing older, acquiring children, never certain that standing around like this was having any effect; it would show Belfast shaking off the trappings of the Troubles – the security gates, the armoured cars – sprouting hotels and bars by the dozen.

The final act on the Ulster Hall on Monday night was Therapy?, doing a cover of Stiff Little Fingers' incendiary 'Alternative Ulster' ('alter your native Ulster, alter your native land'), first recorded in 1978. I had joked to my American friend, 'That will one day be our national anthem.'

Thirty years on, admittedly, some of the lyrics sound dated, far, far more dated than they did even a decade ago: 'Take a look where you're living, you've got the army on the street ...' Others, though, are as resonant as the day they were written and none more so than the half-spoken words with which the recorded version ends: 'Go and get it now.'

Guardian, 12 March 2009

Dissidents

It was one of the sound bites of the post-Troubles era, Gerry Adams's retort to the voice from the crowd telling him to bring back the IRA: 'They haven't gone away, you know.' It is now three years since the Independent Monitoring Commission (IMC), set up under the terms of the Good Friday Agreement, declared that the ruling Army Council of the IRA was no longer functional or operational. On 31 March 2011, the IMC itself bowed out, stating that the bedding down of the Peace Process made its continued existence unnecessary. Two days later a booby-trap bomb was detonated under the car of Constable Ronan Kerr, a murder claimed this Good Friday by a group styling itself the IRA – not, as in the case of previous acts, the Continuity IRA, or the Real IRA (who in a statement on Sunday accused the Queen of war crimes) – *the* IRA.

Gerry Adams says he has no idea who these people are and, more to the point, no idea who they *think* they are: they are masquerading as republicans, whatever letters of the alphabet they use to describe themselves.

There can be no doubting his anger, still less Martin McGuiness's: Northern Ireland's Deputy First Minister has won widespread admiration for his condemnation of the killers of Constable Kerr and, before that, in 2009, the killers of Sappers Mark Quinsey and Patrick Azimkar and Constable Stephen Carroll, as traitors to Ireland.

Both he and Adams talk with justification about the lack of a mandate – dissident political representatives have polled poorly in those elections they have contested – but the fact is that there has always been a strain of militant Irish republicanism – Sinn Féin, as we know it today, emerged out of it – determined to carry on the fight on behalf of the people of Ireland, in the face of apathy or even hostility from the people of Ireland themselves. The current pretenders to the initials draw their claim for legitimacy not from the electorate, but from the example of earlier incarnations of the IRA.

Almost midway between the 2009 killings and the murder of Constable Kerr, in May 2010, a memorial was unveiled at Enniscorthy in County Wexford to the 'Edentubber Martyrs': five members of the IRA killed when the landmine they were assembling exploded prematurely in November 1957 during the so-called Border Campaign. When Gerry Adams announced his intention to stand for Dáil Éireann, he chose the site of the Edentubber explosion itself, just south of the border in County Louth. The Border Campaign ended with the recognition by the then-IRA leadership that there was no stomach for further violence. It marked a turning towards politics by the republican movement, which lasted until 1969 and the emergence of the Provisional IRA.

The IRA is not an army, it is a tradition. IRA is a thing we do here, some of us do, when the political going gets tough or just not to our liking. (Some of us do a thing called UVF too;

we have in the past done a great many other things in the name of the state.) All the adherents to this tradition style themselves Óglaigh na hÉireann – 'Irish Volunteers' or 'Soldiers of Ireland' (it is the official name of the Irish Defence Forces, which is a whole other civil-war story) – and they have all committed acts on a par with the murder of Constable Kerr.

We have dignified such events in our recent past, or at least sanitized them by saying that they occurred in particular circumstances, circumstances which our Peace Process will help us all to understand and, if not forgive one another for, at least accept at face value. The implication is that the participants in the conflict were not so much acting as being forced to act: 'history made me do it', the very argument of course that the various Óglaigh new kids (or not-so-new kids) are using now. Even in the most extreme circumstances there are choices to be made.

Martin McGuinness's forthrightness has, as I say, been welcome and refreshing, but someone, sometime soon has to have the courage to say that while the aspiration to Irish Unity was always legitimate, the means employed – the undercar bombs, the vans filled with explosives, the shooting of informers and civilians as well as members of the armed forces – were always wrong. Not unfortunate, not 'to be regretted'. Wrong.

It may not in itself stop this version of the IRA, but it ought at least to put clear blue water between those who really do believe that politics is the only way to effect change and those who believe it is the only way when they have decided for the rest of us that it is.

Guardian, 27 April 2011

PTAMP

It is a bad day, a man once said to me, when you don't learn at least one new thing. (He was admittedly trying to sell me an encyclopaedia, but the point stands.) I am reminded of this flicking through an old notebook and coming across a page with the words 'goose bumps' on it ...

It was a Saturday. The beginning of this suddenly no-longer-young-looking decade.

My daughter, then four, woke my wife and me wanting to know why people didn't get goose bumps on their faces. 'Because they don't have hair on their faces,' I was about to say, until a hand across my chin proved otherwise. 'Actually,' I said, 'I don't know why.'

So, as soon as I was up — and shaved — I sat down with my daughter at the computer (I know, I know — I should have bought that encyclopaedia).

The reaction we know as goose bumps, or horripilation, is indeed the result of our skin's minute *erector pili* muscles contracting,

173

causing hairs to stand on end. When this happens in animals it often has the effect of making the animal look bigger – witness the porcupine. (Whether you would get a fully expanded porcupine if you played it 'Waterloo Sunset' or wiggled a tongue in its ear was, I am sorry to say, beyond the scope of our enquiry.) There are no *erector pili* muscles on the palms of your hand – and looking for them, as we had not yet the wit to say at primary school, is the second sign of madness: we need our palms for gripping heavy objects in the event that our standing-up hair routine doesn't succeed in scaring off would-be attackers; but there are plenty of *erectores pilorum* on the face, even on the face of an inquisitive four-year-old.

On the face, however, the muscles have grown bigger and taken on other responsibilities, such a helping us chew and keeping our mouths shut – a tried and tested defence mechanism here in Northern Ireland. They are also the muscles controlling our facial expressions, principle among them, would you believe, the smile, which in terms of learning something new made that particular Saturday a very good day indeed for me.

I wouldn't say it got better, but, as the initials PTAMP on the opposite page of the notebook from 'goose bumps' again reminded me, it certainly didn't get worse.

I had gone for coffee with Ithamar Handelman Smith, or Itamar Ben Canaan, to give him his professional name, a young Israeli novelist – and mod – at that time living in Belfast.

Ithamar in his first few months in the city had been struck by two things, firstly the similarity of the streets off the lower Lisburn Road in south Belfast to the settings of the 1960s' kitchen-sink dramas on which he had modelled his style – sartorial rather than prose – and secondly the unusually high incidence of Israeli flags and symbols in certain parts of the city and Palestinian flags and symbols in other parts. So impressed had he been by this second phenomenon, in fact, that he was preparing to make a documentary about it for Israeli television;

so impressed was he that he had even come up with a term for it, or borrowed it from another Israeli novelist he knew. He called it — translating roughly from the Hebrew — 'pissing through another man's penis'. PTAMP.

(I am sure there is a gender-neutral variant — UTAPU? — but I fear in this instance the dangly bit is ingloriously apt.)

I can't remember at this remove if PTAMP was me having fun with the Northern Irish love of initials — buy three, get a mural free! — or being unaccustomedly coy. If it was the latter then I clearly learned nothing when I was younger from my reading of Lenny Bruce's *How to Talk Dirty and Influence People*, in particular the passage relating to his arrest for obscenity after a gig at the Jazz Workshop in San Francisco. The very next night Bruce went back onstage and, with the police watching from the wings, replaced each of the syllables of the previous evening's offending eleven-letter word, beginning c and ending g, as he helpfully explained, with 'blah': for three full minutes he asked his audience, male and female, about the practice of blah-blah-blah, which seemed, from the show of hands he asked for at one point actually to be (a) so widespread as to be verging on the universal and (b) very much enjoyed by all involved.

It was, he told the audience, and the police, at the end, the dirtiest show he had ever done. And all with blah.

Which, even if you don't find it funny, does seem to me to illustrate something about the giving and taking of offence and about how it is possible to be saying one thing while all the time thinking or intending quite another, which in turn brings me back to what I am bound, after all, I think, to render in full as Pissing Through Another Man's Penis, and the finding of new channels for old animosities, on the one hand, and, on the other, appropriating other people's sufferings to bolster our own sense of grievance.

Take the line that Northern Ireland pre-1969 was an 'apartheid state' (and it has been repeated often enough in recent times by senior members of Sinn Féin for that line to seem more and more an official party one). Unionist-dominated, discriminatory and, at local-government level, disenfranchising, it undoubtedly was (as many as a quarter of those who were otherwise eligible to vote in parliamentary elections were denied a vote), but – and it is still a big but – *apartheid?* Look up the Grand Apartheid Laws. Look up the University of Ulster's excellent Conflict Archive on the website – CAIN – and its Introduction to the Electoral System in Northern Ireland. Compare. Pause.[1]

That things were as bad as they were is bad enough. We make nothing better by trying to suggest they were worse, borrowing a bigger stick, if you like, with which to say we were beaten, or indeed are being beaten still.

Last summer, after an Orange parade was refused permission to pass along a stretch of the Crumlin Road in north Belfast, marchers and their supporters established a 'Civil Rights' camp in nearby Twaddell Avenue. The last time the words 'civil rights' were in common usage here it was in reaction to the sorts of discrimination that *was* rife under the old Stormont regime. To compare the lot of Protestants in today's Northern Ireland to that of Catholics forty-five years ago is as egregious a misappropriation as 'apartheid state'.

The thought occurs, though, that at least we are beginning to piss through each other's penises.

Who knows, given time, we might even learn to love them as our own.

Now wouldn't that be cause to exercise our *erectores pilorum?*

Faber & Faber's *Thought Fox* website, April 2014

---

1. I would be showing a lack of confidence in my own argument if I did not also point out that Hendrik Verwoerd, the architect of apartheid, was envious of the Northern Ireland Special Powers Act: an atrocious piece of legislation.

James Ellis's Voice

You never regret the funerals you go to, my father-in-law once said to me, à propos of one that I had decided not to drive from Belfast to Cork for.

I didn't know the actor James — Jimmy — Ellis very well. I had met him on a handful of occasions in his later years when he was publishing poetry and stories with Lagan Press, then run by my friend Pat Ramsey. I had gone to the same grammar school as him — Methodist College Belfast — and like his father, mine was a sheet metal worker in the Harland and Wolff shipyard. For the last decade and more I have been living a short walk from his birthplace, just round the corner from St Mark's Dundela, where C. S. Lewis's grandfather preached, and where at noon last Friday Jimmy Ellis's funeral service was being held. And, as well, I had been thinking, and talking, about him a lot lately. I had published a novel at the end of February, *The Rest Just Follows*, which opens with one of the three main characters, Craig,

177

watching an instalment of the *Up* documentary series with his parents. 'Listen to those voices,' his mother says.

'What's wrong with them?' says his father.

'They're all English.'

'So?'

'So you'd think sometimes we didn't exist.'

As I had been saying when I introduced this passage at readings, Jimmy Ellis, as Sergeant Bert Lynch in *Z Cars*, starting in 1964, was pretty much a lone Belfast voice on TV in those days.

His son Toto got Friday's funeral underway by playing the *Z Cars* theme tune on the flute then later, in his tribute, said Jimmy would probably not have been best pleased, firstly by the two bum notes he hit, and secondly by the fact he had played it at all. He did not consider *Z Cars* his best work: *that* would have been in the late 1950s when, still in his twenties, he had directed plays here in Belfast, most notably *Over the Bridge*, Sam Thompson's drama about sectarianism in the shipyard, mounted in the teeth of the Unionist establishment's opposition.

At the service's end the cortege of family and close friends followed a route to the cemetery that took in Jimmy Ellis's former home and primary school in the shipyard's hinterland, took in too Methodist College, where his acting career began, and Queen's University facing it, where he studied English and French. (He was an accomplished translator of French poetry.)

The rest of us, at the invitation of the family, made our way into town to the Europa Hotel, the bar of which had been a favourite spot of Jimmy's, indeed of generations of actors appearing at the neighbouring Grand Opera House.

I decided to walk it. It was Sports Relief Day and I had been asked earlier in the week to do a mile on a treadmill in the foyer of the BBC, which, owning no shoe more casual than a loafer, I had been quietly dreading. I phoned the producer at the BBC and asked if I could donate the distance from St Mark's Dundela into town instead: two and a half miles.

This precise distance was something else I had been talking about recently, as recently as two nights before, in fact, at another reading in Toulouse, introducing a little suite of prose passages that the composer Philip Hammond had asked me to write for his 2012 *Requiem for the Lost Souls of the Titanic*. I had sweated for months over them unable to find a way in – what was there left to say, after all? – until I read somewhere that 13,000 feet, the depth at which the liner lies, was almost exactly two and a half miles: as far as my house from Belfast city centre. And imagined as (on that occasion) I drove into town that huge ship and all its passengers and crew, all their equipment and possessions, falling, past these houses, this shopping centre, that barn-sized all-you-can-eat Chinese buffet, past these houses too, past the higgledy-piggledy peace line, over the river now, past the train station, still falling, all of it, past Friendly Street, the revamped St George's market facing, down May Street, coming to rest finally at the memorial to itself in the grounds of our City Hall ...

That revelatory journey was via the Albertbridge Road. On the day of the funeral I took the alternative Newtownards Road so that I would pass – about a mile from St Mark's – the junction with Dee Street, whose bridge into the shipyard is referenced in the title of Sam Thompson's play. The first week of April sees the opening of a new footbridge nearby, which – to the great delight of all who dream of a future here free of sectarianism – will be named for the playwright himself. Jimmy was to have performed the opening ceremony. (It will be performed instead by another son of a shipyard worker, actor and playwright Dan Gordon.)

After stopping in at the BBC to drop off the pocketful of fivers I had collected from friends outside the church as sponsorship, I finally arrived at the Europa, about an hour behind the bulk of the mourners, and the same again ahead of the smaller group who had gone on to the interment, which, I only then learned, had been in the churchyard of Castlereagh Presbyterian Church, built in 1835 by a young architect, John Millar (a character in another novel of mine), on a site close to the seat of the O'Neill clan's ancestral home, the so-called 'Eagle's Nest'. Steeped in history doesn't come close: the place is saturated ... and beautiful.

At some point, as afternoon tipped into evening, a screen was lowered in the room where we were all gathered, overlooking Great Victoria Street and the Crown Bar (*Odd Man Out*, and all that), and Toto took to the mic again to introduce a montage: family photos and home movies interspersed with scenes from his father's films and television series, stills from those first school plays. When the screen disappeared again the microphone remained, for anyone, Toto said, who wanted to pay a tribute or share a memory. Several people did: James Greene, fellow actor and school pal, Douglas Fielding, a *Z Cars* co-star, Jimmy's first wife, Betty ... I kept wanting to say something myself, but I couldn't quite get the words straight in my head, or rather my mouth. Even when I have not spent several afternoon hours in the convivial surroundings of the Europa Hotel I can *never* quite get the words straight in my mouth, which is in large part why I write. So of course as I was sitting on the bus home (two and a half miles was enough walking for one day), I worked out what it was I wanted to say. It was to do with that famous TV role, but it related too to the earlier theatre work, the willingness to speak out: Jimmy Ellis gave us a voice, gave us confidence in our voices, and more than that an example of how our voices might be used.

To 'you never regret the funerals you go to' I would add you never regret the opportunities you take to say something, no matter how muddled or inchoate.

I regret that I didn't say it in the Europa. I just wanted to say it now. Thanks, Jimmy.

Arts Extra, Radio Ulster, 8 April 2004

Meditations on the Lost Souls of the Titanic

(Written to accompany a new requiem, by Philip Hammond, performed in St Anne's Cathedral Belfast, 14 April 2012.)

(I)

So this is how the end begins ... That first plunge, as stunningly cold as a face in the basin on a winter's morning, whisking breath away, opening a door on the boy who stepped out – winter summer spring fall – under the vastness of a Midwest sky along the road to school and all that school would lead him to, *summa cum laude* on *summa cum laude*, commodities, country club, every step then an adventure, every foot fallen now a recapitulation of futures past. I can see it with my eyes shut: the wind making waves in the wheat, the farm's small craft flung far and wide, because space like time we had in spades.

Two and a half miles, 13,000 feet: from porch to porch, from surface to seabed, from the beginning to the end of the end.

(2)

CQD CQD SOS SOS CQD DE MGY MGY[1]
Two of us always two of us
CQD CQD SOS SOS CQD DE MGY MGY
In tandem or rotation
CQD CQD SOS SOS CQD DE MGY MGY
The windowless Marconi Room
CQD CQD SOS SOS CQD DE MGY MGY
Tap-tap-tap tap tap tap
CQD CQD SOS SOS CQD DE MGY MGY
Latitude 41.46 North Longitude 50.14 West
CQD CQD SOS SOS CQD DE MGY MGY
Seek assistance. Immediate assistance
CQD CQD SOS SOS CQD DE MGY MGY
Repeat, repeat, assistance
CQD CQD SOS SOS CQD DE MGY MGY
Two of us always two of us
CQD CQD SOS SOS CQD DE MGY MGY
The water-filled Marconi Room
CQD CQD SOS SOS CQD DE MGY MGY
In the sea, clinging, two of us
CQD CQD SOS SOS CQD DE MGY MGY
And then
CQD CQD SOS SOS CQD DE MGY MGY
Just me
CQD CQD SOS SOS CQD DE MGY MGY

---

1. CQD was the international distress call, superseded by SOS, which was used for
    the first time the night the Titanic sank. MGY was the Titanic's own identifier;
    DE is simply 'from'.

(3)

Belfast, says J. B. Doyle in his *Tours in Ulster: a Hand-book to the Antiquities and Scenery of the North of Ireland*, published ('With Numerous Illustrations, Chiefly from the Author's Sketchbook) in 1854 by Hodges and Smith of Grafton Street, booksellers to the university, Belfast creates a very different impression on the new arrival than does Dublin, 'not only in its general aspect, but in the ordinary deportment of its citizens. The easy, promenading air of the citizens of Dublin contrasts rather unfavourably, in a business point of view, with the active bustling of the Northerns. Here men seem to have something of importance to attend to, and to go about it in right earnest.' A bit broad, J. B. Doyle, but not entirely without foundation. Whether it is building things, or tearing them down, bringing harpers from every corner of the kingdom, welcoming a Queen with *Erin go Bragh and Céad Míle Fáilte* misspelt in dahlias, or braining one another with cobbles hoked out from the ground beneath our feet, we manifest a singleness of purpose that would scare you. From one week to the next – one day, one hour, one breath – the worst of people and the best.

(4)

Oh, my honey, oh, my honey, if you could only see me, in my raincoat and my muffler, here on deck, torn between keeping time and trying to keep my feet.

Oh, my honey, my honey, honey lamb, if I could only see you to explain, why I couldn't just 'jump ship', turn my back on the gig.

The order came to play and we played, but that was twenty minutes from the end of yesterday, and here we are, two hours into today, waltzing and ragging.

Not for Black Brothers[2] who will bill you, I will stake what's left of my life on it, for damage to the suit.

Not for the White Star Line, who made passengers, second-class, of us, not crew.

Not even any more for those on whom the awful truth is dawning that there will be no other dawn.

We are playing now for one another, brothers of the AMU, for all whom work has thrown together, Liverpool dockers, Rhondda miners, Massachusetts textile workers, for the family of Anna LoPizzo, for roses as well as bread.

Oh, my honey, oh, my honey, if you could only see me, in my raincoat and my muffler here on deck, I like to think you'd blow me a kiss and dance.

(5)

Because of what we hit we missed the trenches, the Crash, the hungry thirties, the Blitz, the camps, the Bomb. We missed Chaplin, Keaton, *Birth of a Nation*, we missed Jolson, Garland, *Gone with the Wind*. We missed TV. We missed Dixieland and swing, be-bop, hard bop, we missed Elvis, Little Richard, a wop-bop-a-loo-bop, pompadours and mop tops, and wondering what the world was coming to. We missed birthdays, wedding days, anniversaries, christenings and communions, we missed the other fates we might have met, the deaths we might have died, the influenzas, the cancers, the embolisms, the cirrhoses,

---

2. Black Brothers was a Liverpool agency, which had recently won the contract for supplying musicians to the White Star Line in the face of opposition from the Amalgamated Musicians' Union (AMU), whose members as a result became second-class passengers instead of crew.

the suicides, the simply slipping into sleep. We passed instead into myth, launched a library full of books, enough film to cross the Atlantic three times over, more conspiracy theories than Kennedy, ninety-seven million web-pages, a tourist industry, a requiem or two.

We will live longer than every one of you.

Irish Pages, April 2012

Poll Panic

Some time in the course of the afternoon of 18 September I started to experience shortness of breath, dizzy spells. By late evening, when the tremors set in, I was pretty sure I was on the verge of a full-blown panic attack. I recognised the symptoms, having wound up, early last year, attached to a heart monitor in the Ulster Hospital midway through the penultimate episode of *Breaking Bad*. My wife recognised the symptoms too (she it was who phoned the taxi that took me to the hospital that night; I mean, she could hardly leave the children, and there was still half an episode to go). Not only recognised them, but was able to put her finger on the cause. It's the referendum, she said. You've been getting more and more worked up as the week's gone on.

My wife wasn't in Belfast, scarcely yet in the world, in March 1973 for the Northern Ireland Sovereignty Referendum, aka the Border Poll, which presented voters with the choice of a Northern Ireland within the United Kingdom and a reunited, fully independent Ireland. Time may have coloured my memories (as it is already hand-tinting Thursday last: dizzy spells? Tosh), but I close my eyes and I clearly see a scaled-down version of me, with scaled-up trouser bottoms, shaking like a leaf in the school playground ahead of the vote. No one in my increasingly loyalist area had bothered to tell me that nationalists were boycotting the poll and that the outcome – UK OK – was a foregone conclusion. I really thought this could be it, the end of the world as I knew it, with its constitutional guarantees and its irrefutable mathematics: six (counties) into thirty-two won't go.

That was then. I have spent a large part of the forty years since refuting the notion that because I am Protestant by birth I am Unionist by political inclination. If I might be forgiven a grandson-of-Sam moment (*'Vous etes Anglais, Monsieur Beckett?'*), *'au contraire'*.

And yet, my wife was right: the Scottish referendum and the prospect of a Yes vote had shaken me. And this despite the fact that, in Edinburgh the month before for the International Book Festival, I had realized that almost all my Scottish friends – writers who I greatly admired and had been inspired by – were pro-Independence. One of the highlights of the festival for me was William McIlvanney reading from his superb 'Dreaming Scotland' pamphlet, an NHS centred call to vote Yes. And I have to say, sitting in my hotel room later, waiting until the end of the main evening news, from London, for the two-minute round-up of 'regional' Scottish happenings, it all looked pretty Yes to me.

Then I came home again. There's no getting away from it, it skews the way you see things living here. There has of course always been a special connection between Northern Ireland – or the north-easternmost part of the island, to be historically accurate – and Scotland. Their coastlines at the closest point are only twelve miles apart. I grew up with stories of Presbyterians in times past rowing from one to the other to attend Sunday services. For the less zealous, Scotland has long been our point of entry to the Other Island: we have come at England through the west of Scotland ferry ports: Campbeltown, Ardrossan, Stranraer, Cairnryan.

Northern Ireland with an independent Euro state to the South and an independent Euro state – potentially – across a short stretch of water to the east could not but have looked – and felt – a little squeezed. More immediately, a significant amount of the colour would have drained from the Union flags in which the city, or certain sections of it, abounds. Hence the members of the Orange Order from here showing their solidarity by joining with 15,000 of their Scottish brethren and sistren (it's not all boys, you know) in a march through Edinburgh the Saturday before the referendum.

A bar on the Falls Road meanwhile paid for a pro-Independence billboard. Graffiti artists on the eve of the poll climbed halfway up Black Mountain – visible from almost anywhere in Belfast – and painted 'Yes Scotland'.

So we had people who believe in the political unity of the island of Ireland supporting the political partition of the island of Britain, while people who supported the continuing partition of Ireland tramped the streets in defence of the unity of Britain. But it's not the same, they would both say, in much the same way as pro-Independence Scots have distinguished between their 'civic' nationalism and other forms of nationalism. (I'm humming the Smiths here, 'Hand in Glove', 'no it's not like any other love, this one's different because it's us.' But, then, nationalism … Morrissey … Moving swiftly on.)

In my own house the referendum was discussed more or less daily: would we need different money, and would there be an actual border, or just different road markings? my younger daughter wanted to know, displaying a knowledge of Irish political geography sadly lacking in the three young women who boarded the bus I was on recently from Belfast to Dublin airport, emptying the carry-outs they had brought with them so fast that they had to ask the driver to let them off to pee behind a decorative wall at the 'border', which was actually the toll bridge at Drogheda, about forty miles into the Republic of Ireland.

Earlier this week I was at Belfast's Lyric Theatre for a new production of Stewart Parker's *Pentecost*, first staged in 1987, but set in May 1974, a year after the Border Poll, during the Loyalist Workers' Strike that brought down the previous attempt at power-sharing here. As a reminder of how absurd, as well as tragic, things were then in this small corner of the world ('Lilliput', one character calls it), *Pentecost* is without equal. A couple of friends I was chatting to afterwards told me they'd better go before their car was clamped. At least, I said – referencing a line from the play – you don't have to worry any more about it ending up the centrepiece of a barricade. And they both stopped and looked at me. 'Don't jinx it,' they said.

In its ruefulness their reaction reminded me of conversations I had last Friday, abroad in the town, with three separate friends from, as we say, 'different backgrounds', each of whom volunteered the opinion that a Yes vote could have meant things kicking off here again.

As it is, Sinn Féin has since last week turned up the volume on its calls for a new Irish Border Poll. Martin McGuinness, our Deputy First Minister, thinks a debate as 'exciting and enthralling' as the Scottish one is possible here.

Well, it's one possibility.

I ought to say my thoughts on the referendum were not entirely Northern-Irish-centred: I lived in England in the 1980s, and always thought it was the better for its being conjoined with Scotland, Wales too, that Britain at its idealistic best was greater than the sum of its equal nation parts. And it is of course not the people of Scotland's concern what we in our immoderation might do to one another now or in the future; but I blush to say that all that shaking the night of the vote was pure Belfast dread.

Until Clackmannanshire declared.

If only every *Breaking Bad* episode had a moment like that.

Guardian, 27 September 2014

Quietly

Sometimes the right play, or novel, or poem, comes along at exactly the right moment. Michael Longley's 'Ceasefire', published within days of the IRA's 1994 'complete cessation of military operations', springs to mind: 'I get down on my knees and do what must be done/And kiss Achilles' hand, the killer of my son.'

Quietly by Owen McCafferty, which has been playing for the past week in the Abbey Theatre, ahead of a month at London's Soho Theatre, is a revival (it was first performed in Edinburgh in 2010), but it had never until last month been staged in McCafferty's native Belfast, where it was received by audiences almost as a new play.

The play dramatises the meeting in a Belfast bar of two men, both aged fifty-two. When they were sixteen, one of them, Ian, a member of the UVF, had thrown a bomb into that same bar, killing six men, among them the father of the other man, Jimmy.

Ian has asked for the meeting, Jimmy has insisted on the venue, and the timing, the second half of a World Cup qualifier between Northern Ireland and Poland, is a further reminder of the bomb attack, which took place during a match between Poland and West Germany in the 1974 World Cup.

The play has much to say about how we in Northern Ireland deal with past events, not just whether we choose to kiss the hand, as it were, but whether we will ever know whose hand we are (or are not) to kiss.

I saw it last Tuesday night – having been asked to take part in an after-show discussion – and was thinking as I watched of a line from John Calder's memoir of Paris in the 1940s, *In the Garden of Eros*: 'To tidy up history is to distort it.'

Jimmy, in *Quietly*, desperate to understand what Ian could have been thinking when he threw the bomb into the bar, walks him through the attack frame by frame: 'Joe behind the bar – Aiden and Brendan at either end of it – Paddy, Frank – and my da – sittin round the TV.'

Even that, though, is 'just a picture', not the story. The truth, you could say, happens in real time and in more than one place at once. Any attempt at truth-telling will inevitably be partial. The teller – even the best-intentioned teller – of necessity selects. On occasion this selection will amount to conscious omission. More perniciously, the forms of truth-telling will sometimes be employed in a deliberate attempt to obscure.

In his introduction to *The Road: Short Fiction and Essays* by Vasily Grossman, Robert Chandler describes the difficulties Grossman encountered as one of the first journalists to write about the Holocaust when the official Soviet line was that all peoples had suffered equally at the hands of the Nazis: 'A frequently used slogan – all the more effective no doubt because of its apparent nobility – was "Do not divide the dead!"'

There are echoes in that slogan of the appeal in Northern Ireland that there be 'no hierarchy of victims'. This is not to single out that particular phrase, but rather to suggest that the language of truth recovery (including the words 'truth recovery') has been compromised. Repetition has emptied much of it of meaning. Sentences sound more like stratagems than sincere sentiments.

I voiced some of these concerns in the discussion after Tuesday night's production of *Quietly*. In the course of the same discussion Patrick O'Kane, who plays (brilliantly) Jimmy, the murder victim's son, spoke of a moment in the play where 'truth is superseded by honesty'.

It was a stunning insight into a remarkable piece of work, as well as one of the few useful things I have heard spoken on the subject of truth and the past in the last couple of decades.

Whatever transpires in the next twenty-four hours or so behind the walls of Antrim Police Station, where Gerry Adams is being questioned over the abduction and murder of Jean McConville in 1972, let's hope at least that from now on we get a bit more honesty. An admission from Adams that he was indeed for many years a member of the IRA would be a good start.

London Review of Books Blog, 3 May 2014

Don't Go, Anna Lo

God knows, you don't always have to go too far out of your way to find reasons to be ashamed of this place. Last week served up several more, culminating in the spectacle of our one ethnic-minority Member of the Legislative Assembly, Anna Lo, fighting back tears as she spoke of the racist abuse she has suffered on the streets of Belfast.

Latest figures suggest that racially motivated attacks here are up by a third on last year. In one deeply unpleasant incident at the start of May a Roma man had a bag of excrement thrown in his face as he cycled along the Newtownards Road in east Belfast, the same road along which, in a citywide outpouring of pink, the competitors in the Giro d'Italia cycled a few days later. They cycled too past the constituency office of Anna Lo's Alliance Party colleague and MP Naomi Long, petrol-bombed not once, but twice in recent weeks, attacks linked, like several of the racist incidents, to the UVF.

Anna Lo's announcement that she would not be seeking re-election to the Northern Ireland Assembly was doubly

dispiriting, as just a few days earlier she had polled 44,432, or
7.1 per cent of first-preference votes in the Euro elections, by
a considerable distance the best-ever showing by an Alliance
candidate in Europe. Three years ago she topped the poll in
her south Belfast Assembly constituency with 19.8 per cent
of the vote. She is not just Northern Ireland's but the United
Kingdom's first ethnically Chinese parliamentarian – the first
indeed to have been elected anywhere in western Europe.

Her presence at Stormont, her popularity with voters at
successive elections, is something of which we – as well as she –
ought to be proud.

The events of last week appeared to have robbed us all of
even that.

At noon on Saturday, however, a crowd of four thousand
turned out in front of Belfast City Hall to demonstrate their
support, not just of Anna Lo, but of all members of ethnic and
religious minorities living here.

Critics (in my experience people who weren't actually there)
are in the habit of dismissing such rallies – for it is to the front
of the City Hall that Belfast people tend to go at times of anger
and hurt – as 'unrepresentative', which is code for middle-class.
All I can say is that if Saturday was unrepresentative then it
was unrepresentative in the same way as, say, the anti-Iraq-War
rallies were across the United Kingdom, for the same range of
trade union, anti-fascist, and leftwing banners were on display,
in among the homemade placards and the customised T-shirts,
like the one worn by the twelve-year-old stood next to me: 'I
stand with Anna Lo'.

The biggest cheer of the day was, unsurprisingly, for Anna
Lo herself, who delighted the crowd by saying that she was not
now – as she had suggested she might be earlier in the week –
thinking of leaving Northern Ireland; the second biggest was for
Gerry Carroll, newly elected to Belfast City Councillor for the

People Before Profit Alliance who told us not once but twice, '*This* is what Belfast looks like.'

It wasn't fanciful.

Yes there are still a shocking number of racist incidents here and yes there are still headlines being generated that — even imagining for a minute you wanted to — are impossible to duck.

We can, though, when we are put to it, present a very different face, or a whole lot of very different faces ranged in solidarity side by side.

And on days like Saturday we can reclaim a bit of pride in this place.

London Review of Books Blog, 2 June 2014

Insufferable / Surfable
One week in June 2014

Some weeks, writing, I tell myself I could be anywhere. Other weeks I know I couldn't be anywhere but here. Here as in standing in pouring rain with 7,999 other people in Writers' Square opposite St Anne's Cathedral listening to – or trying to hear (it really is teeming) – speeches condemning the recent upsurge in racist attacks in Belfast, and the outrageous comments of our First Minister in defence of even more outrageous comments by Pastor James McConnell. This is the second Saturday in a row we have been out, or the second Saturday half of us have been out, a crowd of 4,000 having gathered – in sunshine – seven days before at the front of the City Hall, to where today as the rain continues to fall we commence to march. Instead of stopping there, however, we veer off in a loop that will lead us back to Writers' Square. At one point, as we turn right on to Castle Street, a cheer goes up. The head of the demo has met the tail, still making its way down Royal Avenue: a virtual (virtuous?) ouroboros.

A woman behind me tells her friend that her computer is so old it is basically two monkeys banging stones together, which in itself is worth walking around the streets in the rain for.

✳

Barbara Jones is leaving Belfast after two years as Joint Secretary of the British–Irish Intergovernmental Secretariat (you have to stay at least one year just to memorise the job title) in which time she has been a force for nothing but good, bringing together people of all stripes (and checks and polka dots and lesser-seen patterns) at her official residence, as she does once more this Monday evening. The ostensible reason is an announcement by Tánaiste Eamon Gilmore of a new Reconciliation Fund. I see several people I saw at Saturday's protest, as well as politicians and civic leaders. There is talk of renewed impetus in addressing the 'outstanding issues', flags, parades, the past. Something, it seems, may be afoot – two rounds of three-day talks, or perhaps three rounds of two. I am trying to be enthused, but I fear for now I am like Eeyore presented with a piece of damp rag after being promised a balloon. 'You don't mind me asking … but what colour was this balloon when it – when it *was* a balloon?'

✳

Joanne Latimer is over from Montreal writing an article for *MacLean's* magazine on No Alibis, one of Belfast's true independents, a specialist crime-fiction shop (and much else besides), which, even when it opened in the late nineties was bucking the trend, though then the threat was not the internet but the heavy discounting bookshop chains. Joanne is also writing a book about her experience, as a child of emigrant parents, returning to Northern Ireland in the 1980s. Her husband has suggested she call it 'The Second-Generation Shamrock Conflict Club'. We meet in the lobby of the Fitzwilliam, next to the Opera House, a hotel that in the 1980s would have been a compensation claim waiting to happen. We talk among other things (it is one of those conversations) about the rise in crime writing here, a consequence, some argue, of the Peace Process's protracted out-workings, which might beg the question, is a small piece of damp rag (yet to be delivered) actually better for the continued health of our literature than a 'one of those big coloured things' properly inflated?

Might. Shouldn't. Give us our fucking balloon.

*

I end the week where I began it, on Writers' Square, well cutting across it, at any rate, on to Church Street, thence to North Street and Sick Records, a newly opened dedicated vinyl shop as trend-bucking as No Alibis and destined, I hope, for as long a life. If you think the vinyl revival is just selling middle-aged men like me the LPs we long ago replaced with CDs only now in 180g re-mastered format, go and hang out in Sick for an hour or two (and Dragon, and Head). I have come looking for Happyness, which Kenny, who runs the shop in between firefighting in Derry, tells me is not on general release until Monday. Like the monkeys with the stones I would walk a long way to hear a sentence like that.

Walk a long way indeed for the line on the LP I take instead, Crocodiles, *Sleep Forever*. 'One of these days the sun will burn out/ And the rain will come to stay/ And me and my love will surf the streets all day.' ('Hearts of Love')

It could be a long-range weather forecast for Belfast. It could be a mantra for how to live here.

Some weeks this city is barely sufferable, some weeks it's surfable.

Look at me, Ma, I'm surfing, I'm surfing!

Sunday Times, 22 June 2014